THE They think it's all over ANNUAL

D1514636

CONTENTS

EIGHTEEN MONTHS LATER...

THE HOUSE IS FULL. WHERE SHALL I PUT THIS?

IT'S DIFFICULT TO PUT INTO WORDS, DOC. IT'S SORT OF A VAGUE THROBBING SENSATION THAT COMES AND GOES. MAYBE IT'LL BEGIN TO IMPROVE IN A YEAR OR TWO!

THE END OF THE SEASON LOOMS...

THINGS ARE DESPERATE, COACH-SAN. IF WE DON'T BEAT OUR GREAT RIVALS GRAMPUS 9 ON SATURDAY WE'LL BE RELEGATED!

NEVER FEAR, CHAIRMAN-SAN. RINEKER'S TOE IS ALMOST BETTER. IT'S A MIRACLE. HE'LL BE ON THE SUB'S BENCH ON SATURDAY!

CHAIRMAN'S OFFICE

COME THE DAY OF THE BIG MATCH...

OH NO! GRAMPUS 8 ARE 5-0 DOWN WITH TEN MINUTES LEFT!

DON'T WORRY—HERE COMES RINEKER-SAN! HE'S BOUND TO SCORE SIX TIMES IN THE LAST TEN MINUTES!

HE'S ONLY GOT THE KEEPER TO BEAT!

HE MUST SCORE!

RING!

RING!

HELLO, THIS IS WALKER'S CRISPS HERE...

HOW MUCH?

SO LONG, GUYS!

GAZETTE

GRAMPUS 8 TANKED. JAPANESE ECONOMY IN RUINS.

David Gower's ENDANGERED SPECIES

Hi, Dave here!
Most of you probably think of me as a dashing left-handed batsman and a brilliant leader of men. Nothing could be further from the truth. In fact, these days I spend most of my time helping to save the world's endangered species from extinction. Here are just a few highlights from my scrapbook:

Here I am with Perth Zoo's white rhino. In the 5th Test against the Aussies in 1991, I helped do my bit by organising a sponsored run-make! Every run I scored raised £100 for the threatened beast. The zoo said they were very grateful for the £300 donation!

One animal I'm always keen to help out is the endangered Siberian tiger. Every week I send £1000 to some nice Russian gentlemen who are saving a tiger for me. So far I've saved the head, which they kindly sent me in the post.

This little chap is a rare Amazonian terrapin that I helped rescue from a logging development, and named Nigel. He even became a sort of mascot, and accompanied me to cricket matches. On one occasion he actually came in useful, when I managed to mislay my box during a Test against the West Indies. Sadly, his little life ended with a Curtly Ambrose lifter, but I'm sure he felt that at that moment, he had repaid his debt to me.

My biggest challenge as a conservationist was to save this poor beleaguered specimen. I was able to provide expert advice on how to manage John Major's election campaign in 1997. Sadly, despite my efforts, Labour registered 418 seats while the Conservatives totalled just 164, and were forced to follow on.

Next week, I'm off to face my toughest challenge yet – to save Channel 5. So long, chums!

Dave

The 'They Think It's All Over' Do-It-Yourself COMPLAINTS Letter

Delete where not applicable

Dear Sir

As a
- parent of three small children
- committed Christian
- pensioner who died in two world wars
- tiresome Welshman

I would like to register my
- disgust
- horror
- disbelief
- oil tanker in Liberia

at the entirely

unnecessary use of the words
- poo
- knobcheese
- Stoke City
- Peter Temple-Morris MP

on your programme.

I only switched on intending to watch
- The Horse of the Year Show.
- anything but your programme.
- BBC2's sock theme night.
- Anal Holiday (Swedish subtitles).

I am surprised that

a sportsman as
- nice
- clean-cut
- crisp-loving
- overpaid

as Gary Lineker or an athlete as
- stylish
- elegant
- hopeless
- oddly-coiffured

as David Gower should lower themselves by agreeing to be associated
with
- your programme.
- that bald git.
- the hairy fat bloke.
- illegal cock-fighting.

I have also written
- to my local MP.
- to the Director-General of the BBC.
- a slim volume of poetry.
- love letters in the sand.

I demand
- a written apology.
- a brown envelope containing £200 in cash.
- to be detained at Her Majesty's pleasure.
- to be allowed to use sharp objects.

I remain
- Yours faithfully,
- Your obedient servant,
- in here until you let me out,
- a tiresome Welshman,

FILL IN NAME HERE

PS Please could you send me a signed photo of Nick and the lads?

Spot the three celebrities in each picture.
Answers overleaf

I think it's Prince William's first night at Eton.

Is it Deirdre Barlow?

I think it looks like the Milky Bar Kid just after a good kick in the knackers.

I would say the whole picture is Gazza and he still doesn't know how to use a condom.

It looks a bit like Duncan Goodhew on a cold day.

It also looks like the bottom half of the face has been out in the sun more than the hands, so it's Mike Atherton.

He's the Lloyd Webber brother who got the looks.

It's Navratilova's new girlfriend, isn't it?

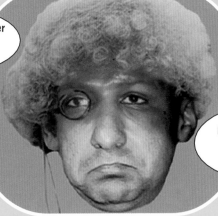

ANSWERS

HAIR
Stephen Hendry, the man whose face comes with free garlic bread.

EYES
Martina Navratilova, on top of Fatima Whitbread there. In her dreams, obviously.

MOUTH
Fatima Whitbread, who failed to give a urine sample recently because she had an erection.

HAIR
Gary Lineker, a box jellyfish at Portsmouth Sealife centre, who's been given that name by the staff. Lineker the jellyfish now has pride of place – in the tank next to Linford the giant winkle and Fatima the bearded clam.

EYES
Paul Gascoigne. Gazza's son is growing very fast. Only last night, Sheryl said, 'Look, he's starting to focus' and the baby said, 'Give him another black coffee then.'

MOUTH
Ray Illingworth, with his finger up his nose. He made a better job of picking that than he did picking the England squad.

HAIR
David Gower, when he was known as 'the Fifth Stylistic'.

EYES
Chris Eubank, who usually wears a monocle, because he's too embarrassed to go to the opticians and ask for 'thpectaclth'.

MOUTH
Ossie Ardiles, Great player, crap manager. Just like Graham Taylor. Apart from the 'great player' bit.

SPOT THE DIFFERENCE

Below are two pictures of England's top team Manchester United in action. But in the lower picture our artist has included ten deliberate mistakes. Can you spot them?

THE MODERN

Every modern training shoe is a scientific marvel. Gone
7/6d – now you can pay up to £129.99 per shoe for

There is a comprehensively designed range of shoes available for every conceivable activity:

FOR CROSS TRAINING:
Air Pro

FOR TENNIS:
Air Sampras

FOR HIJACKING:
Air Jordan

FOR SIGNING ON:
Air Scouse

FOR HANGING OUT ON A STREET CORNER WITH A MOBILE PHONE LOOKING HIGHLY SUSPICIOUS:
Air Tupac

FOR POPPING OUT TO BUY THE SUNDAY PAPERS: Air Popping Out To Buy The Sunday Papers

FOR THE UNDER-14s:
Air Gun To The Head Until You Hand Them Over

FOR EMLYN HUGHES:
Air, I'll Have No.2 Please David

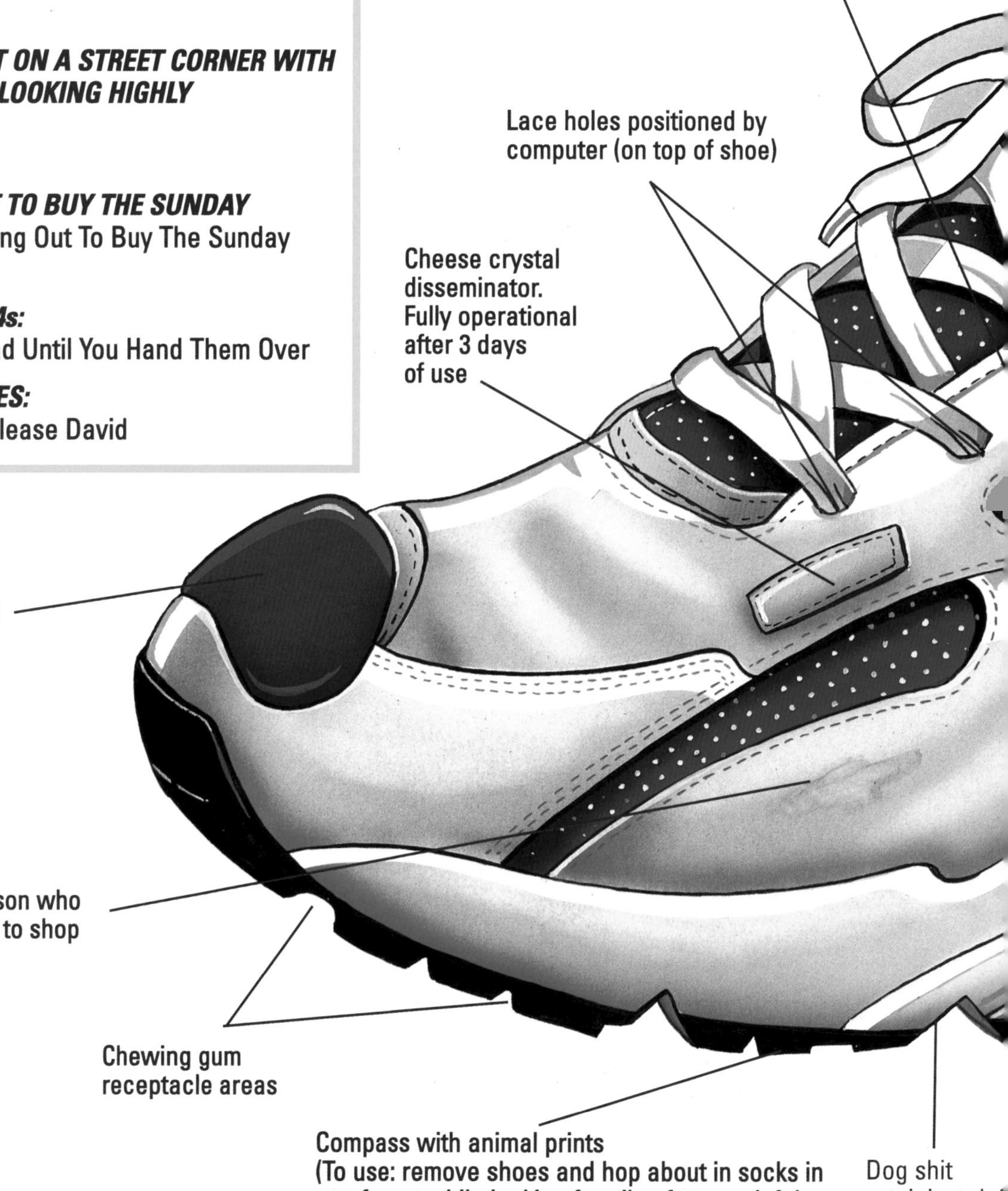

Airflow™ netting handwoven by 4-year-old Vietnamese child doing 18-hour day in windowless room for 5 dong

Lace holes positioned by computer (on top of shoe)

Cheese crystal disseminator. Fully operational after 3 days of use

Driver's airbag

Scuff made by person who brought shoe back to shop before you

Chewing gum receptacle areas

Compass with animal prints
(To use: remove shoes and hop about in socks in wet forest while looking for pile of stones left by Scoutmaster luring you to secret rendezvous)
NB: discontinued 1973

Dog shit retaining clef

TRAINING SHOE

re the days when a pair of pumps set your parents back
n array of sophisticated price-enhancing features.

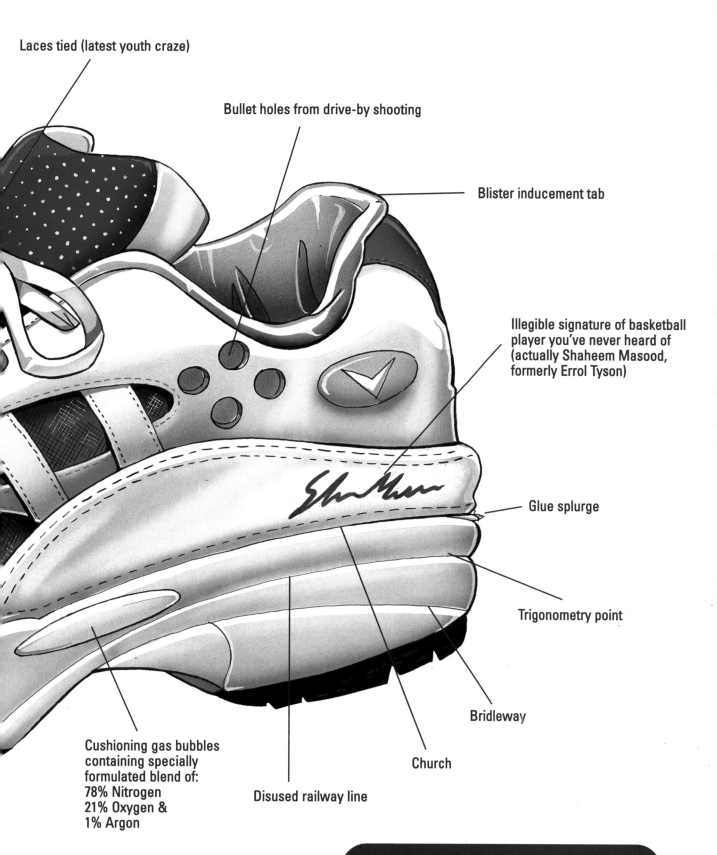

Laces tied (latest youth craze)

Bullet holes from drive-by shooting

Blister inducement tab

Illegible signature of basketball player you've never heard of (actually Shaheem Masood, formerly Errol Tyson)

Glue splurge

Trigonometry point

Bridleway

Church

Disused railway line

Cushioning gas bubbles containing specially formulated blend of:
78% Nitrogen
21% Oxygen &
1% Argon

Great GOAL Celebrations of the World

Goaaaal

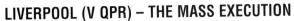

BEBETO/BRAZIL (V HOLLAND) – CRADLING THE BABY

Brazil's Bebeto celebrated not only his goal but the birth of his baby son, with team-mates Romario and Mazhino. Curiously, there were three of them celebrating: presumably no one was sure who was the father. Bebeto comes from an extremely large Catholic family, thus demonstrating that not all Brazilians have a great sense of rhythm.

LIVERPOOL (V QPR) – THE MASS EXECUTION

Apparently, for a bit of light pre-match viewing, to get themselves in the mood for the game, Liverpool had been watching that video of real-life executions, and thought it might be a bit of a hoot to recreate one on the pitch. Those loveable Scousers. A laugh, a song and a mass execution.

The week before they'd been watching 'Brookside', and tried to bury Robbie Fowler under the patio.

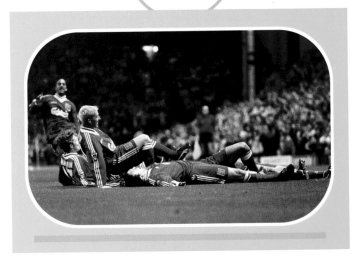

WIMBLEDON (V LIVERPOOL) – AEROPLANES

Wimbledon were taking the mickey out of team-mate John Scales, who'd been refused permission by the Club to take flying lessons, on the grounds that he was too valuable a player to risk. Curiously, Vinnie Jones had been encouraged to take flying lessons – and parachute lessons, and bungee jumps.

It was a pretty amazing sight though – Vinnie Jones still on the pitch at the end of the game.

AYLESBURY (V KINGSTONIAN) –
THE DUCK WADDLE

Aylesbury were living up to their nickname, the Ducks, by waddling. Their next celebration was even more elaborate, in which they basted each other with honey and hung by their arses in the window of a Chinese restaurant.

It's no fun being the Ducks. The first time they brought on the orange segments at half-time everyone panicked.

FINIDI GEORGE/NIGERIA (V GREECE) –
THE PISSING DOG

Before the match, the Greek manager had criticised African football in general and Finidi – Fido to his mates – was demonstrating the kind of shower he'd like to treat him to. In a later game, he scored a hat-trick and tried to shag someone's leg.

He's a great bloke, but you could never get him in the bath at full time. He now plays in Europe, but he only signed on condition that they bought him a little tartan coat to wear in the winter.

STEVENAGE BOROUGH (V HEREFORD) –
THE BALLET

The Stevenage boss, quite simply, had brought in some ballet dancers to train his team in suppleness and agility. Stevenage beat Hereford and went on to face Home Counties North in the next round.

You don't often see footballers in tights – not unless the Arsenal squad go out and do a bank job.

THE KENNY DALGLISH STORY

IN HIS OWN WORDS

WULL, McGLASGIE NAE HIMINY HOMINY WEE BOY BRAW HOOTEN STOOTEN WI KILTS FUR GOALPOSTS THON SHUGGLE FAE PISHT. OOR DAD WHEESHT SLEEKIT 'EAT UP YOUR PORRIDGE' SNAE FRABBIT CRAW DOON CAL 'DINNAE TALK WITH YOUR MOOTH FULL' WHEESHT DRICH. GILLY GANG DROON FROM MUCHWICHT!

SPEN HOOSHT GRICHT PROON CELTIC CELTIC CELTIC CELTIC CELTIC; AIN GRIDDLE SPON McGROOTY BEN GROCHT LIVERPOOL LIVERPOOL LIVERPOOL LIVERPOOL LIVERPOOL; BRIG GRIDDOCK AFT CLOOTY MANAGER'S JOB. AYE, WULL, OOOL GLUM BRUCK PRESSURE, PRESSURE, OH, NOOO, ARSENAL TWO-NIL WINNERS AT ANFIELD FRASSIN' RASSIN' RICK RASTARDLY OCH DRIBBLE KLOOTY CANNAE STAND THE PRESSURE THON SPEN BRIGG OFF MA HEED AN ROOND THE BEND. MUCHTY LICHTY ROUND OF GOLF WI MAE GLIN CASUAL KNITWEAR GAWK PISH.

WULL, SPRAW GRICHT AIN MANAGER'S JOB AT BLACKBURN. BRIGG NOO HOOSHT SPON WI CANNAE STAND THE PRESSURE CRAW AUCHERMUCHTY DONE A RUNNER AN DRICHT LOST IT COMPLETELY; GILLY FRAE ROOND OF GOLF NAE WHEESHT PINK ELEPHANTS WIBBLE WIBBLE MEN IN WHITE COAT WHUPPEN SKRIMMINY THE NOO. AH WEEL.

DROOL McWHIMMINY HIDDLY HODDLY DIRECTOR OF FOOTBALL WHISHT PLUCKET WHATEVER THAT MEANS. SPON GILLY FRAE NEWCASTLE UNITED BRIGG WUP MORE MONEY THAN SENSE.

FRAE KILLTY CLOOTER YON PETER BEARDSLEY! GRICHT HUPPEN NO OIL PAINTING DRIK WHEESHT THE NOO! MACWHUPPIT TRAE HOLLOM FRAE PISHIT OOOR PRESSURE, MORE PRESSURE, OH NOO IT'S STARTING AGAIN, FRANNOCH, NURSE, NURSE! NURSE!

ALAN SHEARER

An exciting new soccer strip in the sun

ENGLAND HAVE REACHED THE WORLD CUP FINAL

IT'S A GOAL FOR ALAN SHEARER!

THAT'S HIS THIRD THIS MATCH!

WELL DONE ALAN!

IN THE PUB THAT NIGHT

ISN'T THAT ALAN SHEARER?

YES!

ALAN IS INVITED TO NO.10 DOWNING STREET

CONGRATULATIONS, ALAN — THERE'S A VERY SPECIAL PERSON WHO WANTS TO SPEAK TO YOU!

TONY BLAIR

ARISE, SIR ALAN!

GAZZACAPP

D'YEE SEE THE JUGS ON THAT NEW BARMAID, GAZZA?

AYE, CHRIS — CHAMPION KNOCKERS LIKE

NOT AS BIG AS MINE THOUGH

OR DANNY'S

TOO *Posh* TO SCORE

♥ *A photo love story* ♥

Young soccer star Dave Beckham has been chucked by his girlfriend...

Sob! Don't do this to me Louise out of Eternal!

Sorry Dave, but I have found another. I'm in love with Peter Beardsley.

What will you do if his looks fade?

I'm sorry, but my mind's made up.

He turns to his friends for advice...

I've been single for half an hour now. What shall I do?

There are many more sardines in the sea – and when you have found the sardine of your choice, you must give it one.

Thanks Eric! I feel a whole lot better now!

But where am I going to meet another internationally famous pop star? Wait a minute, what's that notice?

Wow! What a stroke of luck!

SLAPPERS NIGHTCLUB

Friday

Internationally Famous Pop Star Night

One Night Only

Single footballers welcome

HANCOCK'S HEROES

THE FINEST SPORTSMEN, WOMEN AND HORSES OF OUR AGE

HANCOCK'S HEROES

THEY THINK IT'S ALL OVER

HANCOCK'S HEROES

23

L. Christie

Linford Christie is quite simply one of the all-time athletics greats. What can you say about Linford that hasn't been said before? He's slow and he's got a small penis.

ISSUED BY

THEY THINK ITS ALL OVER

HANCOCK'S HEROES

THEY THINK IT'S ALL OVER

HANCOCK'S HEROES

12

P. Tufnell

Phil Tufnell, England's long-serving left-arm spin bowler, goes by the nickname of "The Cat". Too much grass and he throws up.

ISSUED BY

THEY THINK ITS ALL OVER

HANCOCK'S HEROES

THEY THINK IT'S ALL OVER

HANCOCK'S HEROES

8

J. McEnroe

Wimbledon star John McEnroe married Tatum O'Neal and flirted with an acting career – he had a small part in Ryan's Daughter.

ISSUED BY

THEY THINK ITS ALL OVER

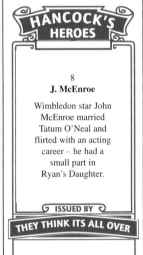

HANCOCK'S HEROES

THEY THINK IT'S ALL OVER

HANCOCK'S HEROES

49

R. Andrew

England and Newcastle RFC's Rob Andrew is known as a gentleman as well as a rugby player. He always lights a lady's farts for her.

ISSUED BY

THEY THINK ITS ALL OVER

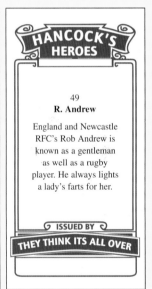

HANCOCK'S HEROES

THEY THINK IT'S ALL OVER

HANCOCK'S HEROES

1

A. Shearer

Much-injured Shearer is England's most expensive footballer, after joining Newcastle for £15 million. He is also a man so dull that he was once in the papers for having a one-in-a-bed romp.

ISSUED BY

THEY THINK ITS ALL OVER

HANCOCK'S HEROES

THEY THINK IT'S ALL OVER

HANCOCK'S HEROES

31

R. Rum

Multiple Grand National winner Red Rum is the only horse to appear in Madame Tussaud's. It's that thing that looks like a dog in the corner. For years, Red Rum trained on Southport beach. He never ran any faster but he became bloody good at French cricket.

ISSUED BY

THEY THINK ITS ALL OVER

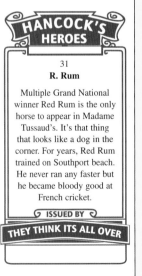

excuses

They think it's all over

GRAHAM TAYLOR

Why, according to Graham Taylor, did England lose to Sweden in the 1992 European Championship?

a) The team had been up all night watching 'Lady Volvo Manufacturers on the Job'

b) The Swedes' outdoor life makes them physically stronger

c) The Manager wasn't up to it

d) Gary Lineker was playing so badly he had to be pulled off.

BEACH VOLLEYBALL

US Olympic beach volleyball favourites Nancy Reno and Holly McPeak were beaten by their own 'B' team and subsequently split up. What reason did they give for falling out?

a) One of them had breast implants and the other disapproved

b) One of them became an Islamic fundamentalist and the other disapproved

c) One of them became a lesbian and the other disapproved

d) One of them wanted to go on the pier dodgems instead.

DAVID JAMES

What was Liverpool keeper David James' excuse for his poor form in the 1996–97 season?

a) He's a Scouser and he didn't want to leave any fingerprints on the ball

b) He thought he was Scottish

c) He'd dyed his hair blue and it was playing on his mind

d) He'd become addicted to computer games which had impaired his reflexes.

NEVILLE MAXWELL

Why, according to Irish rower Neville Maxwell, did he overturn the formbook to win at the Olympics?

a) He'd been drawn in the downhill lane

b) He wanted to get back and watch the beach volleyball

c) He was in a hurry to get home because he'd left the lid off the hamster cage

d) He was the only competitor.

EMLYN HUGHES

Why, according to Emlyn Hughes, did Liverpool lose the 1971 Cup Final against Arsenal?

a) They'd all eaten a dodgy prawn curry

b) They forgot their kit and the referee made them play in their vests and pants

c) Their shirts were too heavy

d) Emlyn was seven at the time.

MIKE ATHERTON

Why, after his dismissal, did Mike Atherton miss the whole of the England 2nd innings against the West Indies at the Trinidad Test of 1994?

a) He blinked

b) He was having his kit drycleaned to get all that dirt out of the pocket

c) He had a quick shower and by the time he came out England were all out

d) He couldn't bear to watch.

answers

NEVILLE MAXWELL (answer: c); MIKE ATHERTON (answer: c); EMLYN HUGHES (answer: c); GRAHAM TAYLOR (answer: b); BEACH VOLLEYBALL (answer: a); DAVID JAMES (answer: d).

WILLIE'S BOOTS

YOUNG WILLIE WILKINS WAS DESPERATE TO PLAY FOOTBALL. BUT HE JUST WASN'T GOOD ENOUGH.

WE'LL HAVE YOUNG HAWKING!

AND WE'LL HAVE LONG JOHN BLUNKETT!

THEY NEVER LET ME PLAY. I'M USELESS. IF ONLY MY GRANDFATHER, THE FAMOUS THIRTIES CENTRE-FORWARD DIXIE LAND, HAD LEFT AN OLD PAIR OF BOOTS IN THE ATTIC THAT WERE SOMEHOW IMBUED WITH MAGICAL PROPERTIES!

Later...

MUM, STOP!

YOU CAN'T THROW THESE AWAY. THESE MUST BE MY OLD GRANDFATHER'S BOOTS, ALMOST CERTAINLY IMBUED WITH MAGICAL PROPERTIES!

NO, SON, THESE ARE THE BOOTS I MARRIED YOUR FATHER IN. THE ONES YOU WANT ARE IN THE ATTIC.

In the attic...

IT WEIGHS A TON!

AYE, IT'S SOLID LEATHER. NONE OF THIS NAMBY-PAMBY AIR RUBBISH!

Willie scores another fifteen goals before half-time.

OUT THE WAY, SAMBO!

But in the second half...

I DON'T BELIEVE IT!

WILLIE'S MISSED A SITTER!

URK! I DON'T FEEL TOO GRAND, LADS.

GASP! HE'S COUGHING UP BLOOD!

PASS ME FAGS, LADS. I'LL BE ALL RIGHT AFTER A WOODBINE.

That night...

IF IT WASN'T SO HIGHLY IMPLAUSIBLE I'D SAY HE WAS SUFFERING FROM THE FIRST STAGES OF TUBERCULOSIS.

FOR HEAVEN'S SAKE, WILLIE, WILL YOU TAKE THOSE BLOODY BOOTS OFF!

The next day...

THE GOOD NEWS, MRS WILKINS, IS THAT THE TUBERCULOSIS IMPROVED OVERNIGHT. THE BAD NEWS IS THAT YOUR SON DIED OF RICKETS THIS MORNING.

Has anyone seen me boots? I'm 103 today and I fancy a kickabout.

SOB!

BOYCOTT ON CRICKET

'Ow do. The important thing in cricket is not to get out. Ever. People haven't come to see runs scored, or to be entertained. They've come to see me. Not getting out. All day.

Head down

1. The Yorker
Dig this one out by playing a forward defensive. Play safe. Don't try to score any runs. Ever. Get your head down.

Head down

2. The Inswinger
Play forward to this one and defend it with a straight bat. Don't make the mistake of trying to score off it. Block it. Keep your head down. Always.

Head even further down

5. The Googly
Get your head down. Always. Block it. Don't move. Ever. Stay still. Remember your average.

Head down

3. The Bouncer
Get your head down and defend it. Don't budge an inch. And whatever you do, don't try and score. Leave that to the other fellow. If he calls for a quick single, don't move. Ever.

Head further down

4. The Full Toss
This is the easiest ball in cricket to score off. Don't. Defend it. Ignore the sound of seats banging up and exit doors slamming. And remember – get your head down.

You are the ref

You're at Old Trafford.

The match is into the 92nd minute. Manchester United are 1-0 down. Do you:
   a) Blow for full-time as the match is over?
   b) Check with Alex Ferguson and wait until Manchester United have equalised?
   c) Trip up the nearest player and award a penalty to Manchester United?

A Manchester United player falls over in the opposition's penalty area. No other player is near him. Do you:
   a) Award a penalty to Manchester United?
   b) Award a penalty to Manchester United?
   c) Award a penalty to Manchester United and send the opposing team's goalkeeper off?

This is your view of a crucial decision in a Liverpool v Arsenal match. Do you:
   a) Retire from football as your eyesight is substandard?
   b) Ask Mrs Elleray to buy you a new pair of glasses?
   c) Consult the Russian linesman?
   d) Award a penalty to Manchester United?

author author

All sportsmen make mistakes during their careers, but nothing so catastrophic as attempting to write their autobiography. Who do you think was responsible for the choice extracts below? Answers overleaf.

1
'That night Jon and I went back to my room in the village. Jenny Stoute was there. I had bought an immense bar of Swiss chocolate. I now took this out of my bag, laid it on the bed, and said, "Right, here goes!"
We didn't get much sleep <u>that</u> night.'

2
'For nearly a month now I have been present at my own funeral. It's bizarre to be present at your own death.'

3
'He walked over to where we were talking and grabbed hold of my crotch. "Hey, get off," I yelled. "What do you think you're doing?" "I just wanted to feel how big those balls really are because that lap was unbelievable." That's quite a tribute from your team-mate.'

4
'I decided to take a hot bath, but my anticipated relaxation turned into a nightmare when a swarm of ants started to run around the rim of the bath, trapping me for what felt like ages. I had to keep topping up the water until they decided to go back to their nest, but at least the weight was lost.'

5
'We form the Nerds and the Julios. A Nerd needs no explanation while the Julios, the good-looking blokes in the squad, take their name from Julio Iglesias. The nerds are: Maysie, Heals, Tubby, AB, Me, Tugga, Ziggy, Babsie, Simmo and Pistol. The Julios are: Hooter, Slats, BJ, Billy, Junior, Unit, Warnie, Cracka and Marto.'

6
'It's a recurring problem with me. You name a hotel in England, I'm probably banned from it. I have made a rod for my own back by getting slung out of so many.'

answers

They think it's all over

A:1

Answer: Sally Gunnell – 'Running Tall'

By the sound of it, if the bar of chocolate was a Toblerone, it's no wonder Sally Gunnell was out injured for the World Championships. Gunnell runs for the Essex Ladies' team. And she'd run even faster if she didn't keep snagging the heels of her white stilettos on the hurdles.

A:2

Answer: Eric Cantona – 'Un Rêve Modeste Et Fou'

The title translates as 'A Dream Modest and Mad'; although somehow it appeared in Britain as 'Cantona – My Story'. The book is now available in your local library. It's filed by author, so look under 'W'.

A:3

Answer: Nigel Mansell – 'My Autobiography'

The man doing the grabbing was Riccardo Patrese, and the bollocks in question belonged to Nigel Mansell. If you want to buy it, it's published by Collins Willow. Mansell was famously too fat to fit into his McLaren. He was last seen 9th on the grid at Silverstone in a Renault Espace.

A:4

Answer: Lester Piggott – 'Lester'

Lester Piggott finally retired after a fall at Goodwood. Officials knew he was in trouble when they realised he wasn't mumbling incoherently. Piggott is a great fan of the Queen. He keeps thousands of pictures of her stuffed in his mattress. Of course, now he's retired, he spends a lot of time with his family – bouncing on his grandchildren's knee.

A:5

Answer: Merv Hughes – 'Merv and Me'

Merv Hughes lives with his mum. Now there's a surprise. Australia's cricketers are soon to visit Pakistan, where they face the greatest challenge of their careers. Twenty-one days without lager.

A:6

Answer: Alex Higgins – 'Through the Looking Glass'

Higgins is a man who's beaten all the world's great players. Some of them at snooker. These days, however, he's hardly ever seen at the table. In fact, he's usually under it. Last year they actually named a big storm Hurricane Higgins. It travelled in a zigzag direction and destroyed all the bars in its path.

Great moments from the
Oxford & Cambridge
Boat Race
Down the Ages

1947: Cambridge edge ahead of Oxford

1951: Oxford edge ahead of Cambridge

1969: Cambridge pull back on Oxford, levelling the distance between the two boats until, with a final supreme effort, Oxford edge ahead again

1973: Bad visibility (but no doubt the same sort of thing taking place)

Thrills and Excitement from the World's Top Sporting Occasion!

Dress Your Own CHRIS EUBANK

Style – either you've got it, you haven't got it, or you can't even say it properly. Here's your chance to dress Britain's premier pugilistic peacock in a variety of glamorous costumes.

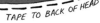

TAPE TO BACK OF HEAD

FOLD   *Nick Davies*   FOLD

Formal Wear
for dinners, banquets, court appearances and retirement announcements

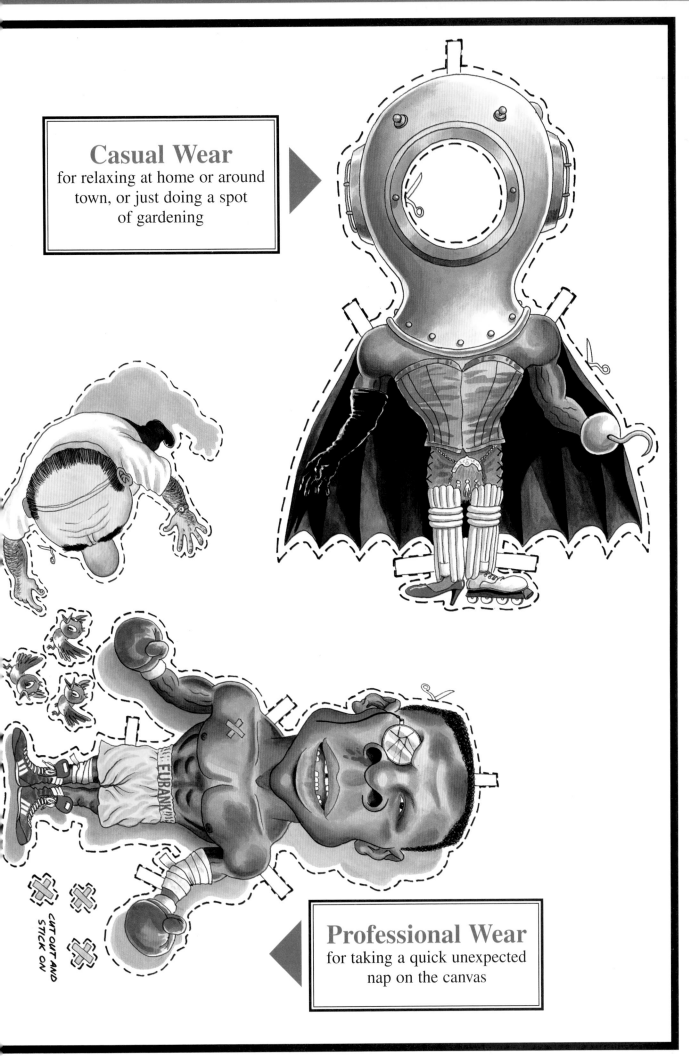

Casual Wear
for relaxing at home or around town, or just doing a spot of gardening

Professional Wear
for taking a quick unexpected nap on the canvas

CUT OUT AND STICK ON

HOWAY!

MAGAZINE • SPECIAL ISSUE • £1.35

MR AND MRS PAUL GASCOIGNE WELCOME US INTO THEIR LOVELY HOME

Villagers in the delightful Scottish hamlet of Glasgow realised that they had acquired celebrity neighbours when they heard the friendly clatter of pots and pans hitting the kitchen wall at 90mph. Soccer player Mr Paul Gascoigne and his lovely wife Sheryl received us in their newly demolished mansion 'Duncartilage'.

The morning we arrived, the Gascoignes had decided to rearrange the decor of their drawing room. The saucepan-shaped indentation in the door is a recent addition. 'Paul prefers the distressed look,' sobbed Sheryl.

Paul has commissioned a small bar area at one end of his dining room, for those quiet evenings in with Fivebellies.

How did you decide upon your son's name 'Regan'?

PAUL: We're both big fans of 'The Sweeney', like, so when the baby was a boy we decided to call it Regan after John Thaw's character. If it had been a girl we were going to call it 'Stripper in bed with Carter'.

What colours have you painted his little nursery in?

PAUL: Don't know. I've never been there, like.

Were you present at the birth, Paul?

PAUL: I don't know. I remember a woman with her legs in the air, but I think that was in London. I also remember calling for plenty of water and hot towels but what happened after we left the Indian restaurant I've no idea.

So tell us about your lovely living room.

PAUL: We've gone for the informal look. We're thinking about knocking it through – another couple of arguments should do it.

What about the smallest room in the house?

PAUL: What do you want to see the library for?

What are your plans for the future?

PAUL: I don't make detailed plans, like, but I expect Sheryl's getting the house, the cars, and the kid. I'll have custody of the lager.

Sheryl, it must be hugely enjoyable sharing your life with one of soccer's premier ambassadors.

SHERYL: Yes.

Paul, I hear rumours that you're a bit of a practical joker.

PAUL: I am that, pet. By the way, did you enjoy your coffee?

Paul, what's your bedroom like?

PAUL: Well, I'm not sleeping there at the moment but the spare room's champion, like.

I don't get home as often as Sheryl would like, like, because wor job means I have to spend a lot of time in night clubs, bars and police custody.

The Gascoignes' sumptuous bathroom is essentially modern in character, but comes with a homely northern touch here and there.

Rupert Murdoch's BIG WIDE WORLD OF SPORT

G'day cobbers!

Rupert Murdoch here. My worldwide revolution in televised sport has already taken in several million people. But it doesn't stop here – not on your nelly. I'm keen to bring many more sports into the 21st century by making them available to a wider fee-paying audience. That will mean one or two minor adjustments to the way some of your favourite sports are played – but I prefer to think of them as improvements!

FISHING Lose the rods and the sleepy fat blokes in wellingtons. Replace the river with a rectangular pitch, with goals at each end. The nets I like. The fish should be rounder – more like soccer balls. Bring in some real beaut cheerleaders too.

HOCKEY Bigger goals, lose the sticks and the ugly sheilas, and make the balls bigger – more like soccer balls. Bring in some real beaut cheerleaders too.

SKYDIVING Lose the parachutes and mount a camera and microphone on the helmet of each skydiver. Mount mid-air goals they have to kick the ball into on the way down. Some real beaut cheerleaders to catch them as they land. This I like.

THREE-DAY EVENTING Come on guys, get real. I say half an hour tops. Lose the horses and the stuck-up toffs. Make the fences into goals and try and get a ball in somewhere. Bring in some real beaut cheerleaders too.

That's my view – but I'd like to hear your views. Phone my pay-per-views line on 01901 930931 and make your contribution. Meanwhile, here's a picture of a naked lady.

PHOTO FITS

Spot the three celebrities in each picture.
Answers overleaf

Is it the reason that Jimmy Greaves gave up drinking?

Isn't that Blakey from 'On the Buses'?

Is that Rory McGrath under incredible G-forces?

It's Freddie Mercury's sister, this one.

Bruce and Anthea's love child?

Is it Des Lynam when he was in Yes?

Is it Russia's first supermodel?

It's the pretty one from 'Prisoner Cell Block H', isn't it? No seriously, it's Sally Gunnell.

Which part, which part?

All of it.

ANSWERS

HAIR
Graham Gooch (although since it's a transplant it really belongs to a Mr Reginald Jeffries of Carshalton).

EYES
Nigel Mansell, the only man who goes to Nick Faldo for charisma lessons.

MOUTH
Greg Rusedski, who's finally proved that he is a British tennis player at heart, by getting knocked out in the first round of the French Open.

HAIR
Steffi Graf, who has won Wimbledon six times. Although, according to her dad, she's never got beyond the first round.

EYES
Brian Moore, who started out as a hooker and now makes a fortune from soliciting. You'll find his law firm advertised in most telephone kiosks.

MOUTH
Sam Torrance, who in the wacky world of golf is known as 'Mr Crazy', on account of the fact that he keeps a pencil behind his ear.

HAIR
Andre Agassi, from the period when he was going out with Barbra Streisand. At Wimbledon that year, he came on Concorde.

EYES
Sally Gunnell of Essex Ladies, who traditionally start their races 'On your marks, get set, go like a train'.

MOUTH
Henry Cooper, who is now 63. So a comeback and an eight-fight series for Sky beckon.

J**O**inthed**o**ts

1 **2** **3**

FOR A PLEASANT SURPRISE

• 1
• 3
• 5
• 7
• 9
• 11
• 13
• 15
• 17
• 19
• 21
• 23
• 25
• 27
• 29

• 2
• 4
• 6
• 8
• 10
• 12
• 14
• 16
• 18
• 20
• 22
• 24
• 26
• 28
• 30

GREAT *SOCCER* VIDEOS

Out Now!

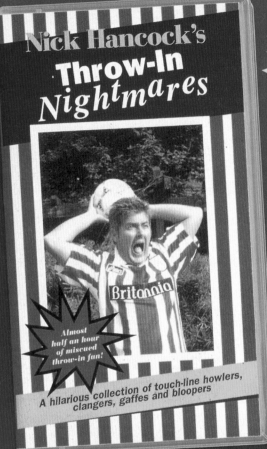

**NICK HANCOCK'S
THROW-IN NIGHTMARES**

Includes:

Mark Hateley (QPR) – *Not his team's throw in*

Trevor Cherry (Leeds) – *Steals 10 yds and ordered to retake*

Stig Inge Bjornebye (Liverpool) – *Doesn't throw it very well*

Linked by the hilarious star of TV's 'Holding the Baby'.

**MICHAEL FISH'S
MATCH ABANDONED NIGHTMARES
Over 250 matches**

Includes:

Rotherham 0   Halifax 0 (1974)
(abandoned 37 mins, hail)

Swindon 0   Oxford 0 (1985)
(abandoned 6 mins, waterlogged pitch – includes full referee inspection)

**...and the never to be forgotten
Lincoln 0   Torquay 0 (1968)**
(abandoned 21 mins, floodlight failure)

FREE WITH EVERY PURCHASE!

DANNY BAKER'S LAST MINUTE PRESENT

A collection of out-takes and disappointing footage, considered not good enough for last year's Danny Baker video.

Includes:
Dog almost runs on pitch, Arsenal 1981.

Ref momentarily looks at wrong wrist, Halifax 1984.

Mis-spelt advertising hoarding, Tranmere 1991.

THE LUTHER BLISSETT STORY

An in-depth 90-minute look at the career of one of England's finest soccer exports. (Subtitled from the the Italian. Originally released as: *'Il Bastardo Expensivo Inglese Qui Non Puo Bottare Una Porta Di Barno.)*

GREAT WELSH WORLD CUP VICTORIES

Includes:

Wales 1   Luxembourg 0 (1961)

Wales 1   Malta 0 (1978)

Wales 0   Iceland 0 (1982)
(Not technically a victory but the goal disallowed in the 42nd minute was miles onside.)

Holland 7   Wales 0 (1996)
(Not strictly a victory but worth watching for a keenly won throw-in in the 82nd minute.)

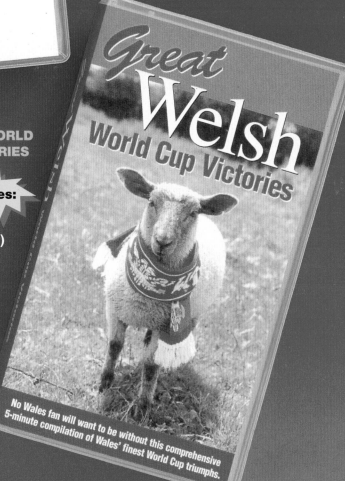

No Wales fan will want to be without this comprehensive 5-minute compilation of Wales' finest World Cup triumphs.

Great GOAL Celebrations of the World

Goaaaa

PAUL GASCOIGNE/ENGLAND (V SCOTLAND) – THE DENTIST'S CHAIR

A satirical response to tabloid coverage of the famous 'dentist's chair' drinking incident in a Hong Kong nightclub, during England's pre-Euro '96 tour of the Far East.
At Euro '96, of course, football came home; had a quick browse round the Sock Shop in the departure lounge; then caught the first plane back to Germany.

WATFORD (V WIMBLEDON) – THE DEAD ANT

This was a recreation of the Dead Ants dance, the best known scene in the film that the team had watched the previous night, 'National Lampoon's Animal House'; although they stopped doing it quickly when Vinnie Jones appeared with a kettle of boiling water. It was a good job that they hadn't been watching '9 1/2 Weeks'.
Watford enjoy recreating scenes from the films of John Belushi, whereas Paul Merson likes to recreate his home life.

SHREWSBURY (V SCUNTHORPE) – THE BIGFOOT WALK

The Shrewsbury players lined up behind scorer Richard Scott in celebration of his enormous feet. And you know what they say about men with big feet. They're incredibly difficult to buy shoes for.
Famously, at Shrewsbury, whenever the ball is kicked out of the ground, it's fetched by a man in a little boat – which is fine when it lands in the river, but it's a bugger on the by-pass.

BARI (V LAZIO) – THE TRAIN

Bari's train impression was brought from South America by their Colombian star, Miguel Guerrero. 'The Train' is now officially encouraged in Italian football as a non-confrontational, non-aggressive goal celebration.

Apparently, a British team here tried to do 'The Train'. They stood around for half an hour, got incredibly pissed off, and then decided to do 'The Taxi' instead. It's not clear, though, what's so original about doing a train. Millwall fans have been doing trains for years.

GRIMSBY (V WIMBLEDON) – INFLATABLE FISH

Grimsby fans went through a phase of holding up inflatables in homage to their club mascot, Harry the Haddock (although in fact they could only buy inflatable rainbow trouts). These days, of course, you don't see many inflatable fish in Grimsby. They've all been pinched by inflatable Spanish fishermen.

Grimsby actually made promotion to Division 1 a few years ago. But they weren't big enough, so they were thrown back.

PETERBOROUGH (V COLCHESTER) – SITTING IN THE STANDS

The Peterborough players decided to christen the club's new stand by being the first to sit in it during this Auto Windscreens Shield Southern Section Quarter-Final. Auto Windscreens have a long association with football – apparently, Tony Adams has been keeping them in business for years.

Peterborough and Colchester are both close to the fens – which, incidentally, is what David Gower calls the supporters.

THE ENGLISH TOURIST BOARD'S GUIDE TO
STOKE

Come to STOKE, and enjoy a holiday in one of Britain's cities. With its two canals, Stoke is often described as 'The Venice of the Midlands' and is the ideal place to enjoy a trip on one of its two canals. Situated in the heart of the mid-Midlands, Stoke is one of the Midlands' famous Spar towns, boasting five Spars, two Costcutters and a Budgen.

Whether it's entertainment or canals you're after, there's always so much to do in Stoke. Meet new friends at the Hanley Road Bus Shelter; witness a fight near the all-night kebab van; or take a short trip to Stoke's peaceful suburbs and watch the cars go past on the M6. For lovers of architecture, why not take a stroll back in time through the quads of the historic North Staffordshire Polytechnic Engineering Department, founded in 1962 (now Stoke University). Or for a long, leisurely day out simply watching the world go by, why not try bus spotting? There are seven numbers to choose from – if you're very lucky you may even catch a glimpse of the rare No. 45B.

Stoke is just famous for its pottery. It's been said that wherever you are in Stoke, you can always spot an item of locally made pottery, or see a local person who has recently used some pottery, or who has at least spoken to someone else earlier that day who *has* used it. Why not take one of the many guided tours available and visit one of Stoke's many pottery outlets, such as BHS, the Reject Shop, or Kwolity Krokkery?

ACCOMMODATION

B & B – Mrs Butterfield, 316 Greasley Road. Traditional Bed and Breakfast served in a friendly atmosphere (Breakfast available 6.00am to 6.05am only. No dogs. No children. No unmarrieds. No newly weds. No ginger hair.)

Hotel Accommodation – Manchester Airport Hotel. For those wishing to treat themselves to a little more luxury, Manchester Airport Hotel is a mere two hours drive from Stoke city centre.

AMENITIES

Art Galleries: 0
Libraries: 0
Port Vale: 0
Swimming Pool: 1 (closed)
Bus Shelters: 17
Operational Bus Shelters: 0
Public Houses: 4,962
Skateboard Rink and Leif Garrett Museum: 1
(temporarily closed, 1974–present)

ENTERTAINMENT

• Enjoy an open-topped tour of Stoke by Rolls-Royce. See the sights of the city from Stoke's only horse-drawn Rolls-Royce (roof and engine stolen).

• Sample the bustling nightlife. Stoke boasts Britain's oldest discotheque (average age 47).

• Come and see Stoke City take on the big-name glamour teams. Just some of the teams that Stoke will be entertaining during the 1997–98 season include: Crewe; Bury; Brazil[*]; Port Vale. The club has recently moved to a new purpose-built stadium with more exits.

(* Fixture subject to confirmation)

• Visit the world's largest permanent display of Shopping Trolleys, situated in the Trent and Mersey Canal.

Reticulated   Central axle   Coin retaining

- Take a once-in-a-lifetime trip to the toilet factory in Longton, where you can watch lavatory bowls go by on a conveyor belt (Admission free; can be seen from main road).
- Spend a fascinating day out at Stoke Zoo. Visit the internationally acclaimed wasp house.
- Enjoy an idyllic picnic in Hanley Cemetery. Or sample a taste of the countryside in Hanley Forest Park, sculpted from a former slag heap.

HISTORY

Famous dates in Stoke's history:

1327 Royal Charter granted.

1328 Royal Charter revoked.

1708 Queen Anne refuses to sleep here, and continues her journey by foot to Glasgow instead.

1942 Luftwaffe fly over Stoke, assuming it has already been dealt with.

1972 STOKE CITY WIN LEAGUE CUP.

1989 Declared 'European City of Sewage'.

CLIMATE

Average precipitation: 5.2mm

Average precipitation in nearest phone box: 10.5mm

Temperature: T-shirt weather (–4C)

MAP

Stoke is handy for the following cities: Paris; New York; Tokyo; Islamabad; Rio de Janeiro; Bogota; Stoke.

LOCAL CUISINE

Stoke has developed its own unique subtle blend of cuisine based on the finest cookery from around the world. There are restaurants to suit all tastes, from the Indian cuisine at the Prince of India Balti House to the Indian cuisine at the 600-seat Taj Mahal Balti-Dome. The wide selection of dishes available in Stoke includes Indian, Indian Takeaway, More Indian and Yet More Indian.

MAIN EVENTS IN STOKE, 1998*

January 1st – Pottery Year (event runs until December 31st)

February 7th to 14th – Kiln Week

March 17th – Glaze Festival

June 4th to 5th – 'Stoke In Bloom' Festival. Will Mrs Butterfield's window box win again, or will that new bit of grass on the Smallthorne Roundabout take the prize?

1st week in August – Glaze Festival

Last Thursday of Month – bins emptied

October, November, December – CLOSED

* All events are subject to cancellation when the organisers arrive in Stoke.

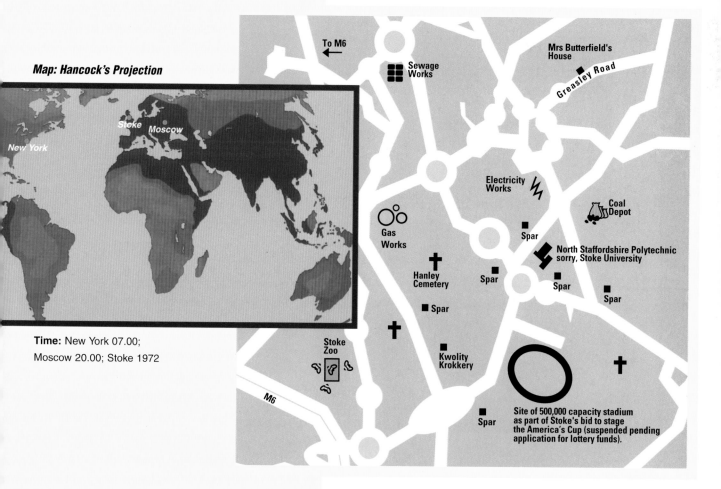

Map: Hancock's Projection

Time: New York 07.00; Moscow 20.00; Stoke 1972

PLAY RORY MCGRATH'S
GOON
THE ARSENA

INSTRUCTIONS:

1) Cut out game. Cut out pieces. Cut out drink. Cut out drugs.

2) Select a counter, and rob it at knifepoint.

3) Each player shakes in turn. Go back on drink and drugs quickly.

4) Throw up a double to start.

5) Each player receives brown envelope containing huge wad of cash.

6) Scarper before the police arrive.

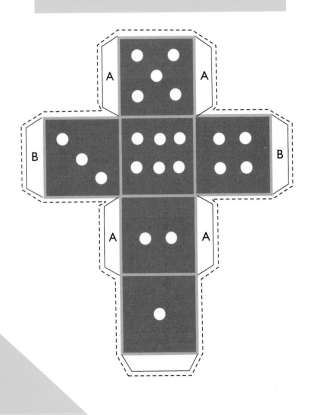

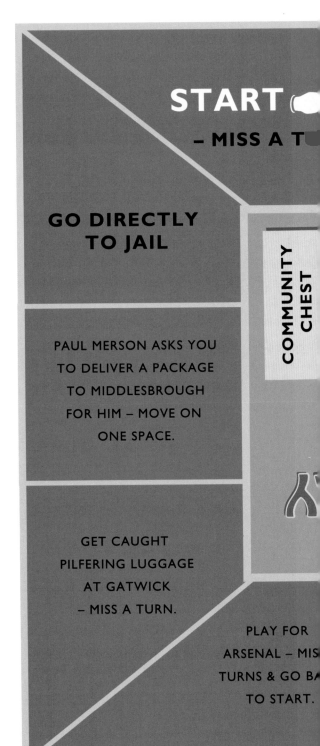

START
– MISS A T

GO DIRECTLY
TO JAIL

COMMUNITY CHEST

PAUL MERSON ASKS YOU
TO DELIVER A PACKAGE
TO MIDDLESBROUGH
FOR HIM – MOVE ON
ONE SPACE.

GET CAUGHT
PILFERING LUGGAGE
AT GATWICK
– MISS A TURN.

PLAY FOR
ARSENAL – MIS
TURNS & GO BA
TO START.

OPOLY
BOARD GAME

from the makers of 'Dungeons and Donkeys'
(ontains small pieces. Not suitable for Ray Parlour.)

ARRY FORMER PAGE THREE MODEL WITH OSTLY DRUG HABIT BACK ONE SPACE.

MANAGE ONLY TWO INTELLIGIBLE SENTENCES ON COMEDY SPORTS QUIZ – MISS A TURN.

MAKE OFF-THE-RECORD ALLEGATIONS TO *DAILY STAR* JOURNALIST ABOUT NEW MANAGER'S SEX LIFE. TRANSFERRED TO GRIMSBY. LEAVE GAME.

GOONOPOLY

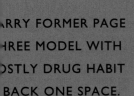

LAST CHANCE FOR IAN WRIGHT FROM FA

TEENAGE BARMAID CLAIMS YOU ARE FATHER OF HER TWIN DAUGHTERS CHERYL AND SHERYL. MISS A TURN.

ACCEPT LIFT HOME FROM TONY ADAMS – GO STRAIGHT TO HOSPITAL.

E WORD 'OBVIOUSLY' 96 TIMES IN ONE MINUTE INTERVIEW OBVIOUSLY GO BACK 4 SPACES.

MAKE ILL-ADVISED DAVID SEAMAN JOKE ON SATURDAY MORNING CHILDREN'S TV PROGRAMME – BACK ONE SPACE.

PIECES
Cut along dotted line

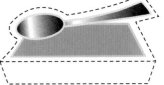
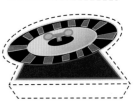

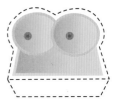

excuses

LENNOX LEWIS

What, according to Lennox Lewis, was the reason that Oliver McCall refused to fight back during their WBC Heavyweight Title decider?

a) McCall's girlfriend was shouting 'Leave it! Leave it! It's not worth it!'

b) McCall was dazzled by Lewis' gleaming white shorts

c) McCall had become a Quaker and had suddenly decided to give up boxing

d) McCall is a big girl's blouse.

TOMMY DOCHERTY

Why, according to Tommy Docherty, did Scotland lose 7-0 to Uruguay during the 1954 World Cup?

a) The game was played in black and white, so it was difficult for the Scots to tell the teams apart

b) The Scots were shagged out after having to stand for the National Anthems

c) The Scots were weakened by the effects of rationing

d) They'd eaten a dodgy haggis before the game.

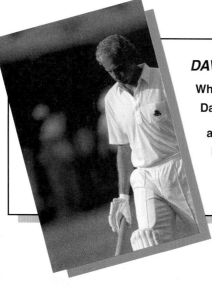

DAVID GOWER

Why, after a disastrous day against Australia in the 1989 Lord's Test, did David Gower walk out of the post-match press conference?

a) He wanted to go and see 'Anything Goes'

b) He wanted to go and see 'Herbie Rides Again'

c) His hair had to be back at the shop by 5 o'clock

d) He was rushing off to be Will Carling's alibi.

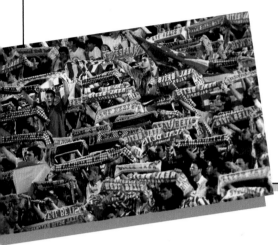

REAL BETIS

What reason did Spanish soccer team Real Betis give for refusing to allow a dead season ticket holder into their ground?

a) Week after week he'd look less like the photo on his ID card

b) He'd smell sweeter than the burgers

c) His ashes were contained in an offensive weapon, i.e. a glass container

d) He'd ruin the Mexican wave.

WOMEN'S RACES

For what reason were all women's races over 100 metres banned from the Olympics between 1928 and 1948?

a) All the starts had to be delayed at the '28 Olympics because none of the women could get ready in time

b) The authorities feared that women athletes would age prematurely over long distances

c) The authorities worried that women wouldn't have time to race and get their husbands' teas ready as well

d) The sight of women's bare legs was considered shocking.

ALAN DAVIDSON

Airdrie keeper Alan Davidson had to miss a key match after confessing to a long-running addiction problem. What did he say he was addicted to?

a) Pickled onions

b) Saturday afternoon films on BBC2

c) Heroin

d) Tomato ketchup

answers

LENNOX LEWIS (answer: b); TOMMY DOCHERTY (answer: b); DAVID GOWER (answer: a); REAL BETIS (answer: c – and it's coming when you can't take a bottle of pop to the game); WOMEN'S RACES (answer: b); ALAN DAVIDSON (answer: a).

A week in the life of JOHN MOTSON

MONDAY

Cornflakes for breakfast, and my goodness me, you have to say what a fine cereal those boys from Kellogg's have come up with there. Today I had 293 flakes, which is 12 up on yesterday but still down on the monthly average.

Today I'm off to Limoges for the Intertoto Cup 2nd prequalifying round replay, which should be most exciting. Thank goodness for the Intertoto Cup, which very much gives the summer some meaning, in footballing terms that is, for it would be wrong of me to imply that the summer is in any way meaningless in a general sense surely. Oh, that and the wife's birthday.

★ ★ ★ ★ ★ ★ ★ ★ ★ ★

TUESDAY

Disaster for Motson. The wife, Mrs Motson that is, is refusing to speak to me. It seems that mysteriously, she didn't entirely appreciate the two surprise tickets to Limoges v Dinamo Plovdiv in the Intertoto Cup. The interesting fact that it was the 14th successive nil-nil draw I've taken her to on her birthday seems to have entirely escaped her. Resolve to cancel those tickets for the Wales v Scotland Schoolboy International.

★ ★ ★ ★ ★ ★ ★ ★ ★ ★

WEDNESDAY

A sad day in the Motson household. I had to take my beloved coat to the vet for a routine check-up. And you have to say, it was not good news, as I may have implied earlier with my reference to sadness, and, of course, days. The vet diagnosed distemper, a severe case of ringworm, and a worrying build-up of Spangles wrappers in the pockets. A shock indeed, although in fairness, you have to say that the coat has never been the same since its 6 months in quarantine following the 1986 European Cup Final (Barcelona v Steaua Bucharest), which curiously enough was also a nil-nil draw, although only after a nail-biting – albeit goalless – period of extra time. Surely.

★ ★ ★ ★ ★ ★ ★ ★ ★ ★

THURSDAY

A disastrous day. No football at all, anywhere in the world. I spent the day in bed with the wife, but remained scoreless – although you have to say it was end-to-end stuff. When interest flagged I tried desperately to maintain my state of arousal by trying to name the members of the 1972 Leeds FA Cup squad – but even this normally fail-safe device tragically let me down on this occasion. My little centre-forward failed to come up with the goods (a reference, I should point out, to the normally reliable 'Sniffer' Clarke of Leeds United FC).

★ ★ ★ ★ ★ ★ ★ ★ ★ ★

FRIDAY

It's the glamour and high drama of the south coast for me as I head for Plymouth Argyle, and what promises to be a fascinating pre-season friendly against Minehead. Minehead FC are something of an unknown quantity for me, as I have only been to see them six times in the last year. My hotel has cable TV and I am pleased to discover a Dull Facts channel. Disastrously however, it becomes scrambled after a mere ten minutes' viewing, leaving me only with channel after channel of free pornography. I complain to the manager.

★ ★ ★ ★ ★ ★ ★ ★ ★ ★

SATURDAY

The best day of the week. There's no other day like it, except sometimes Wednesdays, or Tuesdays occasionally. Oh, and Sundays, and Mondays on satellite, and Fridays if you count the Nationwide League matches. Plymouth's home games are played at Home Park, although curiously none of their away games take place at Away Park. I must remember to inform Mrs Motson of that fact, that is if she's still talking to me when I get back. I arrive at the ground late, my heart pounding, at 8.30am in time for the raw excitement of seeing the white lines being marked out by the groundsman, Ernie Birkinshaw. Ernie is 53 next Thursday, he's a Virgo, a non-smoker, and his blood group is AO. The match itself is a nil-nil thriller, with Plymouth's big no.9 threatening on many occasions although failing to score, as the final result surely indicates, curiously enough.

★ ★ ★ ★ ★ ★ ★ ★ ★ ★

SUNDAY

A great surprise. My coat gives birth to a litter of baby coats. Frankly, this comes as a total shock to me, as I had always thought it was a boy. I return home to discover that Mrs Motson has in fact left, a disappointingly tragic event that is more than made up for by the exciting news that today's live TV game is the all-Premiership clash between Leicester and Derby. You win some, you lose some, and – appropriately enough in the context of this match – you draw some nil-nil.

author

Many sportsmen's autobiographies have been published, some of which have even been written by the sportsmen themselves. But who wrote which of the following passages? Answers overleaf.

1

'All you nasty back-stabbing bastards are going to get your comeuppance. That is what I can promise all those people who have written spiteful things about me over the years. I'm gonna have them. They will be sorted out.'

2

'I wait, and my patience is rewarded. Further down the list is a girl I can afford. She is quite good-looking too; one leg is a bit wonky, but I don't mind that; when I get her home I may be able to sort that out. I put in my bid, and a sale is made. It's the same with horses.'

3

'The only thing I can remember about the match is Bill splitting his trousers when he was playing David and we were leading 6-4. What was worse, Bill doesn't wear any underwear. Normally, he has a very wide stance, but when he was shooting a blue into the middle pocket I could see he was standing with his feet all wrong, trying to squeeze his cheeks together.'

4

'I had received the usual enquiry about my availability to tour India and Pakistan and had subsequently informed the TCCB that I was unable to go. Quite simply, I was afraid for my health, having lost my spleen as a seven-year-old.'

5

'Something very unusual happens today. For the first time in about five years I hand-wash and hoover the cars. I celebrate our six-point lead at the top in style – by creosoting the new fence.'

6

'Standing in the water I shouted, "Hallelujah, I'm clean. Hallelujah, I'm born again." I grabbed Gil Clancy. "Come here," I said, "you're an Irishman, and I love you". I kissed him on the mouth.'

answers

They think it's all over

A:1

Answer: Vinnie Jones – 'Vinnie'

Vinnie Jones keeps ferrets. The ferrets have competitions to see how long they can stay down his trousers.
He was also famously invited to take part in soccer coaching at Eton. He learned basic ball control and passing skills.

A:2

Answer: John Francome – 'Twice Lucky'

Or three times if you count getting the book published.
John Francome has also written fiction – including 'Rough Ride' and 'Stud Poker'.
They sold really well, until people realised they were about horse racing.
Apparently, he had a disastrous wedding night – the going was soft.

A:3

Answer: Cliff Thorburn – 'Playing For Keeps'

The 'Bill' in question was Bill Werbeniuk.
Two Canadians playing snooker – how exciting can life get? Bill Werbeniuk is a Canadian so fat that his left buttock is in a a different time zone from the other one.
No one knows what happened to his underpants, but there was a curious incident in that year's Round the World Yacht Race, when one of the boats had a sail with a rather suspicious skidmark.

A:4

Answer: Geoff Boycott – 'Boycott'

To be fair on Geoff Boycott, he'd actually set off for the airport, then changed his mind and went back, then set off again, then went back… Eventually, he decided he didn't want to spend the winter amongst the squalor and deprivation of India, so he stayed at home. In Barnsley.

A:5

Answer: Alan Shearer – 'Diary of a Season'

A book that makes a useful present for anyone with insomnia.
Apparently, when Shearer scored his first goal for England, he rushed home, hurled his wife onto the bed, and hoovered where she'd been standing.
After the match, when all the lads are in the communal bath, he's the one having a good go at the taps with Liquid Gumption.

A:6

Answer: George Foreman – 'By George'

According to Foreman, God came to him in the shower, after he'd been beaten on points by Jimmy Young. (It was a final eliminator for a title shot against Gloria Hunniford.)
Foreman was so excited that he kissed each man in his back-up team full on the lips.
And at 6'3" and 21 stone nobody was going to turn him down.

HANCOCK'S HEROES

THE FINEST SPORTSMEN, WOMEN AND HORSES OF OUR AGE

HANCOCK'S HEROES

THEY THINK IT'S ALL OVER

HANCOCK'S HEROES

19

M. Tyson

One-time World Heavyweight Champion Mike Tyson is known as 'Iron Mike', because he used to work in the prison laundry. Sky viewers had to pay a tenner to watch the Tyson/Bruno fight, or they could wake up and watch it next morning. That's the option Frank went for.

ISSUED BY

THEY THINK ITS ALL OVER

HANCOCK'S HEROES

THEY THINK IT'S ALL OVER

HANCOCK'S HEROES

74

D. Orchid

Gold Cup winner Desert Orchid was once the nation's favourite horse. He has now retired, and spends his time opening supermarkets. Well, it's nice to meet up with old friends.

ISSUED BY

THEY THINK ITS ALL OVER

HANCOCK'S HEROES

THEY THINK IT'S ALL OVER

HANCOCK'S HEROES

69

HRH The Princess Royal

Princess Anne is a keen Equestrian, and actually won the Horse of the Year Show in 1973. She was particularly strong in the swimwear section. She re-married in 1992. And that time the lucky man was Captain Mark Phillips.

ISSUED BY

THEY THINK ITS ALL OVER

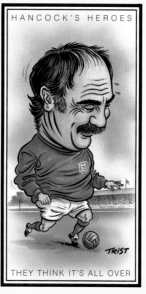

HANCOCK'S HEROES

THEY THINK IT'S ALL OVER

HANCOCK'S HEROES

34

J. Greaves

One of England's all-time great centre-forwards, Jimmy Greaves was controversially left out of the 1966 World Cup Final winning team. And if he ever finds out, he'll be gutted.

ISSUED BY

THEY THINK ITS ALL OVER

HANCOCK'S HEROES

THEY THINK IT'S ALL OVER

HANCOCK'S HEROES

22

J. Torvill

Jayne Torvill won innumerable ice-dancing trophies with her partner Christopher Dean, as well as becoming Sports Personality of the Year: although she's not technically a sportsperson, as all she does is twat about the ice in a frock.

ISSUED BY

THEY THINK ITS ALL OVER

HANCOCK'S HEROES

THEY THINK IT'S ALL OVER

HANCOCK'S HEROES

3

M. Gatting

Former England cricketer Mike Gatting is apparently going to be given extra responsibility at Middlesex next season – he's going to be doubling up as a sightscreen.

ISSUED BY

THEY THINK ITS ALL OVER

'Get into the car.'

Fabrizio Ravioli, Newborough FC's star striker, froze. He knew the voice. It took him back to his native Italy, back to the tiny Sicilian village where he had been born, where he had first learned to kick a football. He had come a long way since then. A very long way indeed.

'Into the car, I said!'

The voice came again, only this time with more menace, more urgency. Fabrizio knew what he must do. Tightening his grip on his training bag, he took two deep breaths as he always did before he exploded over those first few yards. It was his pace that had first got him noticed and now it might just save his life. He narrowed his eyes. He hadn't come this far and scored all those goals for them to catch up with him now. No way. And then, suddenly, everything went black.

It was black too in Roger Fulton's bedroom. Newborough's number one supporter was having trouble sleeping again. All week he'd tossed and turned, unable to stop thinking about Saturday's game. It was Newborough's last match of the season and it was against their arch rivals Chelscastle. The winning team would lift the Premiership trophy, the losers would have to wait four long football-less weeks before even having the opportunity to start trying to get it back. It was almost too much to bear.

Roger abandoned all thoughts of sleep. He'd like as not drop off in Geography again but Mr Fincham was a Newborough fan too and he'd probably understand. It seemed like the whole town was holding its breath until after Saturday. Even Roger's mother, normally as uninterested in football as anyone could be, had asked him if the injured Thomson would be fit to play at the weekend.

Roger switched on his bedside light. His heroes looked down at him from the walls of his bedroom. Stapely. Ringwood. Rousham. Howard. And Ravioli. He fumbled in the drawer of his bedside table and pulled out his most prized possession. An autographed programme from last year's FA Cup Final. Amongst the scrawls of the other players one signature stood out, all graceful swoops, considered angles and Italian style. Fabrizio Ravioli. Roger

ROGER TO THE RESCUE

A SHORT STORY

traced the line of the letters with his finger. No, there would definitely be no sleep tonight.

In the damp cellar, the Italian star striker was also tracing something with his fingers. A large and painful bruise had started to appear high on his cheek and he touched it gingerly. The man sitting opposite him smiled.

'I am sorry for the roughness. Emilio takes his job very seriously, don't you, Emilio?'

The thug standing by the door smiled; an evil smile distorted by the scar that ran the whole length of his right cheek.

'What is it you want from me?' asked Fabrizio.

'Want? We don't want anything. It is surely you who want something. To live, perhaps.'

The man was suddenly serious, his

Sicilian accent crackling in his throat, his garlic-laden breath hot in Fabrizio's face.

'You owe us, Ravioli. The goal you scored in the last minute of the Copa Europa cost us thousands, perhaps millions. This Saturday you will pay your debt. Or it will be the worse for you.'

Fabrizio looked into the man's eyes. It was a steady, unwavering look, a look that so many goalkeepers knew and feared. It was the look he gave them as he placed the ball on the penalty spot, the look they saw as he started his run up. The next thing they knew, the ball was ballooning the back of the net. The man held his gaze for a few seconds and then glanced away.

'Emilio, I think our football star needs another little lesson.'

The thug smiled his evil smile and, pulling on his black leather gloves,

himself as the giant native swung his huge arms over his head to limber up. Ginger looked down the pitch at his sister, Pippa. She smiled bravely.

'Play up, Ginge! Only twelve needed off the over! And if he drops it short on the leg side, smash the fucker into the sea!'

She probably wouldn't have said that last bit, but I do believe in extending the form a little where possible. Anyway, what time is it? Christ, I should have been in the King's Head five minutes ago. Bollocks, where were we? Oh yes, wop in the cellar, refusing to throw key match.

Look, actually I'm not sure I can be bothered to do this in full and the so-called 'editor' is too busy sniffing that new girl in Illustrations to actually read any of it, so do you mind if we kind of 'cut to the chase', as they say?

'Absolutely, old chap, we quite understand,' chorused the understanding readership, thereby earning the eternal gratitude of a thirsty hack.

The noise of the crowd was deafening, but above the shouts of victory from the Newborough fans and the cries of 'Well played, Fabrizio, superb hat trick!' the great man

came towards Fabrizio.

It's amazing. You're actually still reading this. Most people would have given up by now and flicked on to something with some pictures in it.

Actually, there are only two stories in books like these. There's this one: star striker gets kidnapped by evil villains on eve of big match and then rescued by boy fan; and the other one: party of schoolchildren are shipwrecked on desert island and have to beat the local tribe at cricket for a reason which is never totally clear.

Fancy a bit of that one?

Ginger looked down the flattened sand of the wicket at the chief. The chief was smiling, a big broad smile that showed every one of his filed teeth. The smile broadened even further and turned into a grin as he tossed the small coconut they were using as a ball to a huge native with massive shoulders.

'This is our secret weapon Emerson. He hollows out tree trunks for a living. All day with that axe, thwack, thwack, thwack. He's quite quick.'

Ginger felt his knees go weak and he leant heavily on the driftwood bat.

'Eye on the ball, foot to the pitch, only an over to go,' he said to

managed to make himself heard to the group of eager journalists.

'Eeet has always been my drim to play at Wembley and win the FA Cup,' (or was it the Premiership? NOTE: Check before sending piece in.) Fabrizio said in his heavily accented English.

'But I would not haf bin able to do zees today without my friend Roger, who rescued me from very bad men who are now 'elping Interpol with their enquiries.'

Roger felt himself starting to blush as the journalists muttered and looked at him, licking their pencils.

'Therefore, to thank heem, I present heem weeth thees, my FA Cup winner's medal, to keep forever.'

Roger stared at the medal glistening in its silk-lined box.

'Is it really for me?' he gasped.

Fabrizio looked down at him and smiled.

But Roger couldn't speak. He just stared at the medal, HIS medal, given to him by his new friend, Fabrizio Ravioli.

Roger looked at the medal every day from then on. He still looks at it. In fact, he's looking at it right now as it sits on his desk, beside his typewriter. I know, because although I'm a man now, I too was once a boy and a mad keen Newborough FC fan. Called Roger Fulton.

Play FANTASY

The brand new all-in-one fantasy game. Just pick eleven sportsmen from the lists below and follow their progress during the season. Score two points for a goal, a try, a wicket or a place in the 3.30 at Catterick. Concede three points for an own goal, use of the outside arm at a line-out, or an overturned toboggan.

TEAM NAMES

You will need to think of an embarrassingly lame knob pun for your team name, and register it on our 24-hour hotline (£24 per minute peak rate, £28 per minute at all other times. Calls last an average of 2 hours).

CHECK YOUR PROGRESS

Telephone weekly to hear a recorded message telling you that you're no. 219,765 out of 293,241.

TRANSFERS

After a month or two, you may find you wish to transfer your interest to a more rewarding hobby, such as pornography. We recommend *Shaven Havens*, *Wet and Willing*, or *Big Ones Monthly*.

WEST INDIES (CRICKET)

001	Branston Pickle
002	Gladstone Bag
003	Brentford Nylons
004	Wellington Boot
005	Winston Cigarettes
006	Kingston Polytechnic
007	Cumberland Sausage
008	Courtney Fish
009	Valentine Card
010	Bentwood Furniture
011	Sanderson Wallcovering

BRAZIL (FOOTBALL)

012	Junior
013	Senior
014	Plato
015	Aristotle
016	Diogenes
017	Timon of Athens
018	Blind Pericles, the Seer of Old Delphi
019	Scenario
020	Fellatio
021	Patio
022	Brianinho

SRI LANKA (CRICKET)

023	Paxman Persistentquestioninghe
024	Aima Singingindaraina
025	Wende Begindabeginhe
026	Dippa Wicke Wambamthankyoumam
027	Chuckberi Mydingalingsingalonghe
028	Poorol Michaelfinneganbeginnaginhe
029	Youonli Singhwenyourwinninghe
030	Sari Imustbegoinghe
031	Thisara Fewofmifavouritethingshe
032	Brown Paperpackagestiedupwithstringhe
033	Gingang Guliguliwotchagingangoo

WEST INDIES (CRICKET) AGAIN

034	Oswestry Bypass
035	Mornington Crescent
036	Barchester Chronicles
037	Hudsucker Proxy
038	Holcroft Covenant
039	Osterman Weekend
040	Shawshank Redemption
041	Remington Ladyshave
042	Cumbersome Briefcase
043	Levington Compost
044	Witchfinder General

ROWING

045   Steve Redgrave
046   The Other One

YUGOSLAVIA (FOOTBALL)

047   Mild Panic
048   Lemon Harpic
049   Haman Chisandwic
050   Drumma Buddyric
051   Gudmornin Wivanandnic
052   Soluble Phensic
053   Scraczin Jockic
054   Pearlone Dropstic
055   Tonyadams Rodavanoracarinadic
056   Davedi Dozibikimikantic
057   Yo Bic

GOLFERS

058   Greg Normal
059   Ian Sweater
060   Fuzzy Logic
061   Pringle Pringle
062   Laura Bloke
063   Bland Mormon
064   Tiger Feet
065   Bob Hat
066   Kenny Lynch
067   Curtis Weird III
068   Hopeless Japanese IV

HOLLAND (FOOTBALL)

069   Stobart van Leasing
070   Warnink van Reversink
071   Express van Rental
072   Armoured van Robbery
073   Sherpa van Trophy
074   Burgher van Poisoning
075   Obi van Kenobi
076   Guitarist van Halen
077   Curseyou van Helsing
078   Cara van Oflove
079   Koko van Withrice

WWF WRESTLERS

080   The Undertaker
081   The Overtaker
082   The Chartered Surveyor
083   The Door-to-door Encyclopaedia Salesman
084   The Executive Producer
085   The Butcher
086   The Baker
087   The Candlestick Maker
089   Rich Man
090   Poor Man
091   Beggarman Thief

BASEBALL TEAMS

092   San Francisco Irons
093   Boston Stranglers
094   Florida Drive-By Killers
095   Wichita Linemen
096   Virginia Wolfs
097   Tennessee Williamses
098   Texas Homecarers
099   Colorado Beetles
100   Washington Irvings
101   Arkansas Chugabugs
102   New York Mining Disaster 1941

YET MORE WEST INDIES (CRICKET)

103   Bradford Argus
104   Everton Nil
105   Dwight Christmas
106   Lipton Teabag
107   Hogarth Roundabout
108   Courtly Love
109   Anderson Country
110   Pilsbury Doughboy
111   Oscar Nomination
112   Devon Creamteas
113   Evergreen Shrub

YET YET MORE WEST INDIES (CRICKET)

114   Herringbone Tweed
115   Pilkington Glass
116   Argos Catalogue
117   Lincoln Convertible
118   Catford Dogtrack
119   Dashboard Instrument
120   Greenhouse Effect
121   Leamington Spa
122   Rampton Hospital
123   Solsbury Hill
124   Bognor Regis
125   Wishbone Ash

HOLDING THE BABY
- Page 8 -

Scene 7
INTERIOR: HOUSE
NICK IS ROCKING A PRAM GENTLY

Nick: There there, baby I've been left
            holding due to my girlfriend
            running off with another man. I
            wonder where that laddish flatmate
            of mine has got to?

            ENTER LADDISH FLATMATE (WEARING
            FOOTBALL JERSEY AND SWIGGING FROM
            CAN OF LAGER)

Flatmate: 'Ere, that fabulous bird down your
            office that you were chatting up -

Nick: I was not chatting her up.

Flatmate: She said you said you were gay.

Nick: 'Gay'?? No, not 'gay'!!! I said I
            was 'grey'!!!!

Flatmate: Oh no! I've just invited 250 gays
            who are here on a coach trip from
            San Francisco round for a party
            this evening!!!!

            NICK DOES TRIPLE TAKE

Nick: Doh!!! But we can't have a party!
            I've been left holding the baby
            due to my girlfriend running off
            with another man!!! What are we
            going to do???

Flatmate: If only we had a dippy female
            neighbour you could pretend was
            your girlfriend. She could hold
            the baby for you.

            SFX DING DONG

Nick: That'll be the doorbell.

Neighbour: Wow, man! Groovy! I've just come
            from Greenham Common!

Handwritten annotations:

NB: Nick unavailable Tues PM. (Diarrhoea voice over)

EXCELLENT. This is much better than draft vi. Keep diary free for BAFTA ceremony - Producer

Cut shot of Nick looking accusingly at agent in audience

Can we use the word "Gay"? Check with arse bandits upstairs.

SOUND Add big laugh here

SOUND Add huge laugh here too

SOUND Audience to die laughing here please

Make sure he remembers which camera to look at this time.

and here

Unbelievably ma... explosion of hila...

PHOTOFITS

Spot the three celebrities in each picture. Answers overleaf

Is it that bloke who comes up to you in Leicester Square and goes 'minicab'?

It looks like Lyle Lovett after he's just received the divorce papers from Julia.

He's not nice, but I'd give him one.

It looks like Norman Tebbitt's kid sister.

Is that me or the picture?

I think the bottom bit's Claudia Schiffer. After severe hormone treatment, which I will give her.

Is that the reason Lester Piggott wanted a cell on his own?

I thought the eyes were Damon Hill's. But if they were, Schumacher's eyes would have come in and knocked them out.

It's like a human shaving brush, isn't it?

Looking at that hair, I think that's Dave falling down a lift shaft.

It's Don King's hair. How does he do his hair? Come to think of it, how does anybody do their hair?

ANSWERS

HAIR
David Seaman. Can we just make it clear now – officially – that there is absolutely nothing funny whatsoever about his name. Although how he keeps a clean sheet is a mystery.

EYES
Duncan Goodhew, who actually went bald after falling from a tree as a child. Lee Hurst, on the other hand, head-butted a pot plant as a baby.

MOUTH
David Coulthard, who pronounces his name Coul-thard, not Coul-tard. What a thosser.

HAIR
Bobby Charlton, who was a great advocate of the 4-3-3 formation: four hairs at the back, three at the sides, and three scrape'd over the top.

EYES
Damon Hill, who these days tends to finish behind the likes of Pedro Diniz – upside down in the gravel pit on lap eleven.

MOUTH
Boris Becker, who's ginger, and called Boris. Bloody good job he didn't go to my school.

HAIR
The beard of Dr W G Grace, 19th Century cricketer and star of 'Are You Being Served?' The doctor was almost impossible to get out – especially on a wet night in February.

EYES
David Icke, who insisted that God had instructed him to wear turquoise shellsuits. So obviously, the Supreme Being is a Scouser with shares in Millets.

MOUTH
Ian Wright, who has a gold tooth in his mouth. In the Arsenal dressing-room, it's the only safe place to keep your valuables.

J**●●**inthesp**●**ts

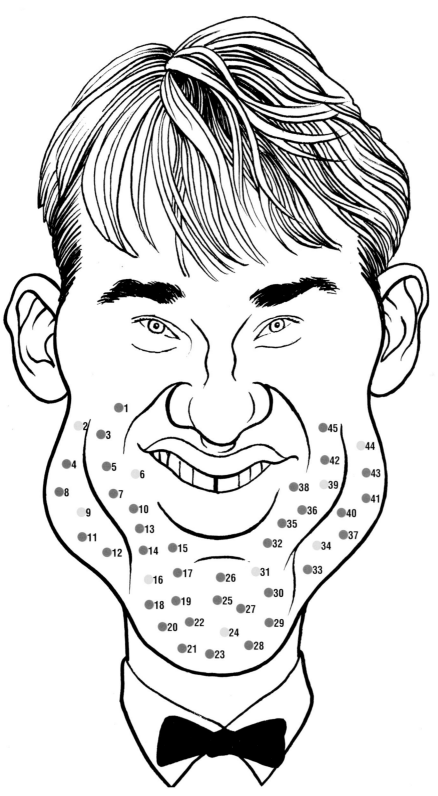

The *WILL CARLING*™ MOTIVATION COURSE

*Hi! I'm Will Carling™. When I played rugby for England, I didn't get out of the way for anyone (except possibly Jonah Lomu). But now I'm **TACKLING** problems of a different kind. My course will **CONVERT** you into a winner, **KICK** your failure into touch and **FEED THE BALL BACK INTO THE COLLAPSED SCRUM** of your success. But don't take my word for it – listen to these satisfied customers...*

'*Our accounts department were thrilled to be allowed to spend five minutes drinking weak lager with Gareth Chilcott.*'

G & L Photocopiers, Basildon

'*We spent our entire last year's profits standing in a field trying to build a space rocket out of wire coat-hangers. We can't thank Will Carling enough.*'

Target Ball-bearings, Huddersfield

Hi! I'm Will Carling™.

What an executive weekend course entails:

Day 1: *Evening:* Reception with stars from the world of rugby (G Chilcott).

Day 2: *Morning:* Assemble in woods in boiler suits, with plank slightly narrower than nearest stream. Addressed for 5 minutes by man with chin like an arse, who then leaves by helicopter for pressing appointment at nearest five-star restaurant. Remainder of exercise supervised by highly qualified ex-SAS* trainer.

Afternoon: Stand by stream shouting at each other. Go back to hotel.

Evening: Get-together in the bar to discuss day's activities. All pick on weakest member of office and laugh when he cries about his father. Sandra from accounts gets drunk and screams at Managing Director that she's having his baby.

Day 3: *Morning:* Honesty session. Managing Director finds out who honestly doesn't like him. Resolves to dismiss them all on Monday morning.

Afternoon: Post-mortem (for Eric from personnel who died of exposure on character-building overnight hike).

Evening: Farewell drinks with top international celebrities from the world of sport (G Chilcott).

(*Southampton Agricultural Supplies)

A photograph of the actual woods you will get lost in (Trees may vary.)

✄------------------------------

TO: **WILL CARLING**™

☐ Yes, I'd like to enrol for the **Will Carling™ motivation course**. Please rush me an invoice for £29,000 (first instalment).

☐ No, I can't be bothered.

As a result of reading this, your name and company name may be passed on to a central Gullibility Register. Tick box according to preference:

☐ Yes, I wish to receive reams of useless junk through the post.

☐ No, I do not wish to pass up this golden opportunity.

GREAT INDY CAR CIRCUITS
OF THE WORLD*

Your cut-out-and-keep guide to the world's great indy car circuits

DETROIT, MICHIGAN

DIRECTION OF DRIVE

RIGHT

WRONG

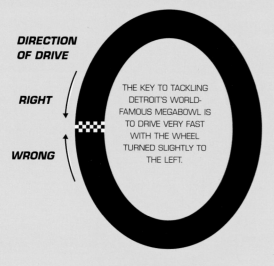

THE KEY TO TACKLING DETROIT'S WORLD-FAMOUS MEGABOWL IS TO DRIVE VERY FAST WITH THE WHEEL TURNED SLIGHTLY TO THE LEFT.

ST. LOUIS, MISSOURI

THE CRUCIAL THING TO REMEMBER AT THE ST. LOUIS INDYDOME IS TO DRIVE FASTER THAN EVERYBODY ELSE AND NOT TO GO IN A STRAIGHT LINE AT ANY POINT.

DES MOINES, IOWA

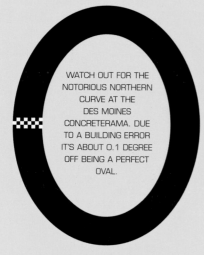

WATCH OUT FOR THE NOTORIOUS NORTHERN CURVE AT THE DES MOINES CONCRETERAMA. DUE TO A BUILDING ERROR IT'S ABOUT 0.1 DEGREE OFF BEING A PERFECT OVAL.

DES LYNAM, NORTH DAKOTA

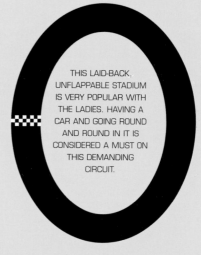

THIS LAID-BACK, UNFLAPPABLE STADIUM IS VERY POPULAR WITH THE LADIES. HAVING A CAR AND GOING ROUND AND ROUND IN IT IS CONSIDERED A MUST ON THIS DEMANDING CIRCUIT.

MOOSEJAW, ALASKA

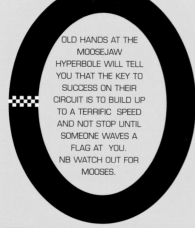

OLD HANDS AT THE MOOSEJAW HYPERBOLE WILL TELL YOU THAT THE KEY TO SUCCESS ON THEIR CIRCUIT IS TO BUILD UP TO A TERRIFIC SPEED AND NOT STOP UNTIL SOMEONE WAVES A FLAG AT YOU. NB WATCH OUT FOR MOOSES.

ONE HAT FALLS, ARIZONA (ACTUAL SIZE)

IF YOU'RE COMPETING AT ONE HAT'S FAMOUS SNOOZEDROME, WATCH OUT FOR THE TRICKY RIGHT-HANDER, FOLLOWED BY A SHARP LEFT WITH REVERSE CAMBER OFF THE MAIN DRAG. THEN, WHEN YOU GET TO THE STADIUM, JUST DRIVE ROUND AND ROUND FOR SEVERAL HOURS.

* COUNTRIES OUTSIDE AMERICA NOT INCLUDED

Great GOAL Celebrations of the World

Goaaaa

SUNDERLAND (V ARSENAL) –
THE BIG NOSE AND BALDY HEAD CELEBRATION

The big nose and baldy head being celebrated belonged to skipper Kevin Ball.

Actually it's fairly easy to score at Highbury – there's usually a dealer in the dressing-room.

Incidentally, Sunderland have moved to a new stadium. Anything to avoid paying council tax.

FARNBOROUGH TOWN (V BARNET) –
THE FREEZE

This routine was based on the end credits of 'Police Squad', in which the cast freezes with the exception of one person. For their next goal, the lads tried a celebration based on 'Inspector Morse'. It lasted for two hours and no one knew what was going on (and the bloke who scored the goal turned out not to have done it after all). Farnborough is in Hampshire. In fact the ground is just at the bottom of David Gower's garden, about sixty miles from his house.

NOTTINGHAM FOREST (V MANCHESTER CITY) –
THE GALLOP

The Forest players were imitating David Pleat's famous gallop across the pitch when Luton Town avoided relegation in 1983.

While manager at Tottenham, David Pleat was officially cautioned for attempting to pick up a prostitute. He's the only man who actually runs faster than he drives.

Forest's caretaker manager at the time Stuart Pearce is nicknamed 'Psycho', because of his aggressive style and total commitment. And not because he keeps his mother's mouldering corpse in the basement.

NOTTS COUNTY (V WREXHAM) – THE LITTLE WAVE

The Football League had sent out a directive to every club asking them to stop doing extravagant goal celebrations; but as County hadn't scored in over eleven hours of football, their chairman said he didn't care what they did if they put the ball in the back of the net. This was their ironic response.

Like Newcastle, Notts County are known as The Magpies – a bird which is notorious for picking up shiny silver objects. And there the similarity doesn't even start.

CELESTINE BABAYARO/NIGERIA (V ARGENTINA) – WOBBLY LEGS

The fact is, that Babayaro was so happy at scoring that his legs gave way, and all the other players thought he was doing a celebration and joined in.

Nigeria, of course, has a terrible human rights record – second only to Wimbledon.

Maradona was banned from that match after failing to provide a urine sample. Mind you, you try pissing half a kilo of solid coke.

CAMBRIDGE UNITED (V WELLING) – THE ELEPHANT

The Cambridge elephant celebration derives from the fact that a number of the squad have enormous ears; but the reason they actually performed it on TV was to appear on 'They Think It's All Over'. It's not at all clear why they thought they'd get on to the programme if they looked like an elephant...

Gary, of course, has never been on safari to Kenya – for fear of being poached. And Lee has never been to a greasy spoon cafe – for fear of being poached.

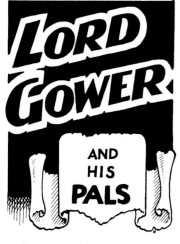

LORD GOWER
AND HIS PALS

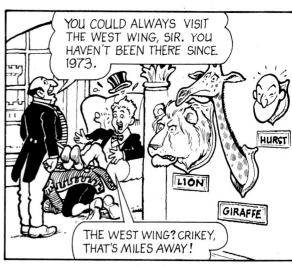

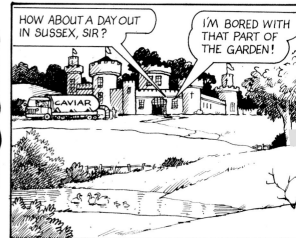

HERE COME THE POOR PEOPLE NOW!

HELLO! AND WHAT DO YOU DO?

NUTHIN' MUCH, MAN.

SO YOU'RE AN ARISTOCRAT TOO, THEN?

AND HOW LONG HAVE YOU BEEN COMMON?

THE GAME BEGINS...

HE'S TAKING AN AWFULLY LONG RUN UP, SIR!

LET'S TEACH THIS RABBLE A THING OR TWO ABOUT CRICKET ENGLISH-STYLE!

THAT'S OUT! TOP HAT HIT WICKET!

YIKES!

CRIPES!

THIS INNINGS

RUNS	0
EXTRAS	0
TOTAL	0
WICKETS	7

I SAY! GOOD BALL!

OOER! TIME FOR A CAPTAIN'S INNINGS. BETTER PAD UP!

HO HO! I KNEW UNCLE ALGY'S OLD SUIT OF ARMOUR WOULD COME IN HANDY ONE DAY.

TEE HEE! THIS'LL SHOW OUR ECONOMICALLY DISADVANTAGED CHUMS WHO'S BOSS!

HOW'S HE DOING, ILLINGWORTH?

WELL, AFTER A PROMISING START HIS LORDSHIP HAS SOMEWHAT PREDICTABLY WAFTED ONE TO THIRD SLIP WITHOUT MOVING HIS FEET, SIR.

DID WE WIN, ILLINGWORTH?

I'M AFRAID NOT, SIR. YOU LOST THE SERIES 5-0, SIR.

HURRAH! BREAK OPEN THE BUBBLY! THAT'S OUR BEST RESULT YET!

THE BRITISH OLYMPIC ASSOCIATON

1 Wandsworth Plain Wandsworth London SW18 1EH

To: Bengt Stigmundssen
International Winter Olympic Committee
Seven Mile Beach
Grand Cayman
West Indies

Dear Bengt,

I was particularly saddened to receive your recent communication rejecting Britain's bid to hold the Winter Olympics in the year 2058. Thank you for the return of our glossy brochure. I cannot begin to convey the sense of frustration and disappointment here at Olympic Headquarters when it was discovered that the phrase 'Go Peterborough 2058' would not be the slogan on the world's lips in the intervening years. In fact so confident of success was our celebrity fund-raising committee (myself, Brough Scott, Carol Vorderman, Les Gray – formerly of Mud – and Peter Temple-Morris MP) that we had already commissioned 200,000 'Go Peterborough 2058' keyrings, displaying an embossed representation of our Olympic mascot Colin the Parsnip behind clear plastic.

It remains a mystery to us why the IOC placed our application behind those from Val d'Isere, Lillehammer, Reykjavik, Lagos and Alice Springs. I would remind you of our many exciting proposals for new events that would have revolutionised the Winter Olympics along British lines:
• Path clearing
• 4 x 400 metres gritting
• Windscreen scraping (with old credit cards)
• Dog rescuing (local pond)
• Pissing your name in the snow at closing time
• Forgetting where your mittens are
• Winter of '63 anecdotes (marathon)

As a country with a proud Winter Olympic tradition (79th in slalom 1932), I would like to point out too that Britain has recently made great strides to compete on level terms with the world's best, and last month lost only narrowly to the Solomon Islands in the qualifying rounds of the mixed luge.

With regard to your meteorological misgivings, I would further stress that Britain frequently experiences cold snaps of the kind required to host such an event. I appreciate that it is impossible to forecast exactly when such conditions will prevail, but in this age of modern communications surely it would not be unreasonable to expect the world's athletes to keep a close eye on Ceefax (p. 401).

I remain, sir, your obedient servant,

R. Rothmans-Yearbook.

Sir Richard Rothmans-Yearbook
Chairman
British Winter Olympics bid

author author

Bored? Cold? Throw another sportsman's autobiography on the fire and try our fiendish quiz. Which sportsman wrote which of the passages printed below? Answers overleaf.

1

'On our wedding night I was glued to the TV. I sat riveted on the end of the bed on the first night of our honeymoon, watching my seven hundred pounds disappear as Costa Rica beat Scotland.'

2

'He grabbed hold of me and threw me up against Cassius Clay. Clay didn't know what was coming. As I bumped into him, Cassius put his hands up and said, "Don't hit me, don't hit me please".'

3

'The unfortunate boy that was killed was standing as umpire. I am glad to say that the players, who were the indirect cause of the boy's death, were in no way to blame.'

4

'By the end of 1989, I had become aware that for a man of my increasing profile, not to mention outstanding good looks, there was an ancillary world worth investigating. This was only a few months after the time when I had scored my first try for the British Lions in Queensland, and a member of the crowd had pronounced: "That boy will never lay another brick in his life".'

5

'Above him stood a 6-foot tall woman dressed in a black leather bra, pants and thigh-high leather boots brandishing a thick leather belt. "You are guilty and now I am going to punish you," she screamed at him as the belt came lashing down on his buttocks. Life had changed dramatically since the early days.'

6

'Today I recorded an episode of the quiz show "They Think It's All Over". Well, now it really _is_ all over, the recording, I mean, I have got to admit that I cheated.'

answers

A:1

Answer: Paul Merson – 'Rock Bottom'

Forty lines a page – that was what Merson was on when he wrote it.
Only last year Paul Merson went to Alcoholics Anonymous and took the Pledge. Followed by the Harpic and the Mr Sheen.

A:2

Answer: Willie Carson – 'Up Front'

Carson's work was actually released as a talking book, read out by Peter O'Sullevan. But the running time was only three and a half minutes.
Two jockeys have actually won awards for writing fiction – Dick Francis for 'Whip Hand', and Lester Piggott for 'Collected Accounts 1980-85'.

A:3

Answer: W.G. Grace – 'Cricket'

W.G. Grace played for Gloucestershire for 32 years. And it still ended in a draw.
Doctor Grace was the only famous sportsman of his time with a knowledge of drugs. Things have really moved on from then, haven't they?

A:4

Answer: Jeremy Guscott – 'At the Centre'

Jeremy Guscott is one of rugby's posher players – he has asparagus ears.
Despite being a top-flight rugby player, he maintains a part-time job with British Gas. He always turns up for training, although he can never say if it'll be morning or afternoon.

A:5

Answer: Bjorn Borg, in Lars Skarke's 'Winner Loses All'

It was Borg who was getting the thrashing from a leather-clad prostitute; although for most players, a glass of Robinsons Barley Water is quite enough between sets.
The equivalent no-holds-barred orgy for a top British player would be a mug of Horlicks and half a Wagon Wheel.

A:6

Answer: John Motson – 'Motty's Diary'

The book lifts the lid on Motty's private life, including the extraordinary story of how he spent his wedding anniversary in a jacuzzi with three Danish hookers. Oh, all right then, he was in Doncaster watching a Pontins League game.

How to play
FEEL THE SPORTSMAN™
in the privacy of your own home

It's easy to play FEEL THE SPORTSMAN™ in the comfort of your own home. Here's what you will need:

- Two teams of at least two people
- One more friend or family member to act as arbiter
- Two blindfolds
- A stopwatch and a whistle
- Two top-class international sportsmen

(**Note:** If no top-class sportsman is available, John McCririck will do)

Lee Hurst's star tip
Suggest everyone wears blindfolds. Then take yours off and nick the video.

David Gower's star tip
When the 90 seconds is up remove your blindfold and shake the hand of the sportsman firmly. Try to disguise the fact that you haven't a clue who the sportsman is, and above all don't speak until the chairman says: 'It's Pele'.

Rory McGrath's star tip
Sniff for perfume. If you smell any, it is probably a woman. Concentrate your searches on the upper chest area. Ignore any slaps or knees to the groin.

Gary Lineker's star tip
Bring a pin with you and use it discreetly to make two small holes in the blindfold, just big enough to see out of. Extra tip: Be sure to do this BEFORE you put the blindfold on.

Nick Hancock's star tip
Stoke City to win the double.
NB. Live animals may cause soiling.
See also rugby players.

ZOLA'S

The 'They Think It's All Over' cameras followed pint-sized soccer superstar Gianfranco Zola on an exciting day as one of Britain's premier sportsmen.

9.00am It's down to the ground for a kickabout!

9.30am I get a call from my agent. These portable mobile phones can be so handy! Strangely, I've never lost this one!

10.10am A quick check on the watch shows me it's only fifty minutes until elevenses!

11.00am With the help of my big chum Juninh we finally get the top off a tube of Smarties. Yum yum!

DAY OUT

2.00pm I go out for an afternoon's riding with my old mate Frankie Dettori. He's the one on the left, riding the Shetland pony.

4.00pm Teatime, and time for a relaxing game of travel chess.

7.00pm Down to the newsagents to buy my lottery ticket. Mr Patel offers me a paper round, whatever that is.

9.00pm Back home to my custom-designed bar. Is it just me, or am I getting smaller?

excuses

ALEX FERGUSON

Why, according to Alex Ferguson, did Manchester United suffer a shock 3-1 defeat at Southampton in the 1995–96 season?

a) The referee hadn't added enough injury time

b) Owing to their outdoor lifestyle, Southampton were physically stronger

c) Manchester United are rubbish

d) The United players couldn't make each other out in their grey away kits.

ALLAN LAMB

What was Allan Lamb's excuse for his remarkable 18 off a single over to win a one-day international against Australia in 1987?

a) He was still on drugs from the night before

b) It was an 18-ball over

c) He's South African, not English

d) Ian Botham had put itching powder in his underpants.

WIMBLEDON

One month into the 1996–97 season, Wimbledon were bottom of the league. Then, overnight, they shot to the top of the table and reached the semi-finals of two cup competitions. Why the amazing transformation?

a) They dropped Vinnie Jones

b) They stopped trying to play stylish football and reverted to kick-and-rush

c) The chairman threatened them with a visit to the opera followed by a dinner of sheep's testicles

d) The chairman promised them all a night out with Linsey Dawn McKenzie.

ESTONIA

The Estonia v Scotland World Cup tie in 1996 lasted just 3 seconds, because the Estonians failed to turn up at their own ground. What was their excuse?

a) They were eating their lunch and refused to leave before they'd had their pudding

b) They got stuck in a horse and cart jam

c) They refused to play on a Saturday because they'd all become Seventh Day Adventists

d) The game clashed with the Estonian potato festival.

STEVE COLLINS

Why, according to Steve Collins, did Chris Eubank lose the WBO Super Middleweight crown to him?

a) Eubank thought that Collins had been hypnotised

b) Eubank thought he'd be fighting Joan Collins

c) Eubank wanted to make everyone happy

d) Eubank had injured himself driving to the fight.

ALAN SHEARER

Why did Newcastle United reject Alan Shearer as a teenager, only to buy him later for £15 million?

a) He was scared off by the sight of Peter Beardsley

b) He was too small

c) They had an introductory chat with him and they all fell asleep

d) They put him in goal at his trial and decided that he was a rotten keeper.

answers

ESTONIA (answer: a); *STEVE COLLINS* (answer: a); *ALAN SHEARER* (answer: d).
ALEX FERGUSON (answer: d); *ALLAN LAMB* (answer: a); *WIMBLEDON* (answer: c);

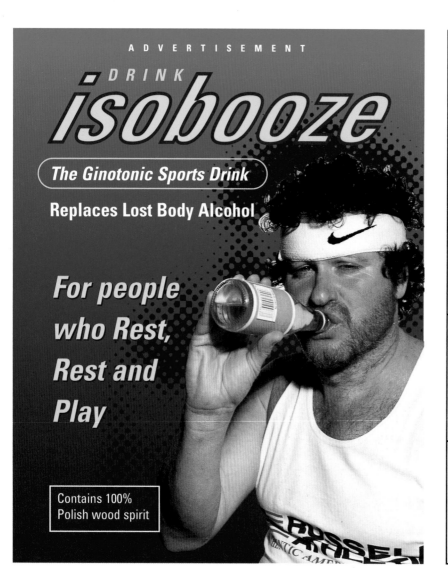

RESULTS

RUGBY LEAGUE

SUPER LEAGUE:
WORLD CLUB CHAMPIONSHIP: POOL A

WIGAN (0) **0**
WOGGA WOGGA (34) **73**
WOGGA WOGGA: Tries: Harris R. 4, Hogan 3, Dundee 3, Tuiga'lets 1, Temple-Morris 1

BRADFORD BULLS (0) **0**
KOONUNGA HILL 3rd XIII (87) **154**
KOONUNGA: Tries: Murdoch R. 9, Minogue K. 4,
Minogue D. 3, Minogue Z. 2, Minogue A. 2, Donovan J. 2, Bushkangaroo S.T. 2

ST. HELENS (0) **0**
BARRAMUNDI PREPARATOR⎯ CONVENT FOR GIRLS UNDE⎯ 14 TEAM (BLIND GIRLS ONL⎯ (126) **238**
BARRAMUNDI: Tries: Farriss J. 11, Farriss A. 8, Farriss T. 7, Pengilly K. 6, Hutchence M. 2, Beers G.G. 2⎯ Oil M. 2

EUROPEAN GROUP

	P	W	D	L	F	A	Pts
Wigan	10	0	0	10	0	762	
Bradford	10	0	0	10	0	1513	
Warrington	10	0	0	10	0	1893	
London	10	0	0	10	0	2214	
St. Helens	10	0	0	10	0	2631	
Halifax	10	0	0	10	0	3426	

AUSTRALIAN GROUP

	P	W	D	L	F	A	Pts
Wogga Wogga	10	10	0	0	3219	0	20
Koonunga	10	10	0	0	2817	0	20
Oggyoggyoggy	10	10	0	0	2101	0	20
Zigazig-ah	10	10	0	0	1647	0	20
Barramundi	10	10	0	0	1323	0	20
Mattress Springs	10	10	0	0	894	0	20

☆ ☆ EUROSPORT ☆ ☆

4th Jan

7:00am Morning Golf with Brough Scott. Another chance to see the All-Milwaukee Women's Golf Championship of 1981.

8:00am One Man and his Crab.

8:30am Indoor Gado-Gado from Jakarta (5-a-side). Renggeng Dangging and Peter Purves bring you the best of the day's action from the Jakarta Gado-Gadodome.

10:00am Bare-knuckle Whittling from Hanover. Siggi Osmundsen (Iceland) v Kurt Slug (DDR). Presented by Gert Hinkelhof, with Brough Scott in the studio.

11:00am Golf World. A further chance to enjoy the All-Milwaukee Women's Golf Championship of 1981. With Brough Scott.

12:00pm Wczyczwltzprymntcz. Live from Warsaw with Brvg Sczot.

12:01pm The World Picnic Championships. Blanket-based action from the Dick Turpin roundabout on the A3, with Una Stubbs.

1:00pm Pro-celebrity Hanging from Iran with Alvin Stardust.

2:00pm International Dusting from Prague. Featuring the J-cloth challenge with Ed 'Stewpot' Stewart. If wet, indoors. If dry, indoors.

4:00pm Golf at Tee-time with TV's Mr Golf, Brough Scott. Action you may have missed from the classic All-Milwaukee Women's Golf Championship of 1981.

5:00pm Pro-celebrity Cottaging from Brighton. Some surprise names join hands under the cubicle door for more exciting hole-in-the-wall action.

6:30pm International Paint Drying (black and white only). Our super slomo cameras make sure you don't miss a second of the action from the Coventry DIY exhibition. Commentary by Kenneth Kendall and Linsey Dawn McKenzie.

7:00pm Speedway (liable to cancellation).

7:00pm International Paint Drying continued. (Speedway cancelled.)

8:00pm Duvet Changing from Limoges. The Queen-sized challenge (9-tog professional category) with Chris Kelly and Julia Carling.

9:00pm Junior Topiary. Under-15 hedge-clipping highlights from Helsinki with Nik Kershaw and Peter Temple-Morris MP.

10:00pm Budgie-baiting from Spain. Controversial live animal cruelty event with Michael Rodd.

11:00pm Comedy Zone. A sly, sideways look at the week's news with Parsons and Naylor.

11:02pm Late Night Golf. Another chance to see today's edition of 'Morning Golf' with Brough Scott.

The Grand National
Fence *by* Fence

Your cut-out-and-keep guide to the horse-lover's favourite race

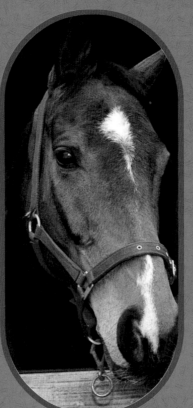

Fence No. 1
The Electric Chair
'Joyful Prince' strained ligaments 1990. Sold to French restaurant 1991

Fence No. 2
The Gluepot
'Certain Winner' broke all four legs 1986

Fence No. 9
The Brick Wall
cunningly painted to look like open countryside. 'Splendid Chance' killed outright 1978

Fence No. 3
The Executioner
'Sprightly Lad' broke neck on impact 1991

Fence No. 8
Carnage Turn
'Sole Survivor' and 'Immortal Lad' impaled on fence 1981

Fence No. 4
Hanratty's Drop
'Cheerful Chap' and jockey Bob Luckless shot by race marshals 1967

Fence No. 7
The Dull One
No horses killed. Yet.

THE MELLING ROAD ('Lucky Boy' run over by margarine lorry 1979)

Fence No. 5
Vet's Delight
'Forever Young' put down by lethal injection 1975

Fence No. 6
The Meat Wagon
Sponsored by Pet-O-Chunks. Six horses and three animal-rights protesters killed in pile-up 1994

CONCOURSE

WORLD CUP '98
A SPOTTER'S GUIDE

The craze for face painting is sweeping the globe. Every fan is doing it. Here's a handy at-a-glance guide to enable you to identify who follows whom.

ENGLAND

IRELAND

WALES
(not painted, just embarrassed at doing so badly)

SAUDI ARABIA

INDIA

SEVERE MEASLES

AMERICA

AMERICAN INDIAN

AUSTRALIA

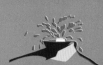

IRAN

BELGIUM

USA
(South)

AMAZON

ENGLAND
(rugby)

GLASTONBURY

ALADDIN SANE

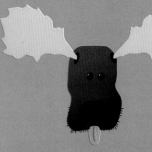

CANADA

CLOWN

HANNIBAL LECTER

JOHN THE BAPTIST

PHOTOFITS

Spot the three celebrities in each picture.
Answers overleaf

The hair is Tony Adams: he came out of the pub, fell asleep in the gutter, and they painted a yellow line over his head.

Is it the face that Gary chose out of the plastic surgery brochure, so that Vinnie Jones wouldn't recognise him?

No, that's after Vinnie Jones got hold of him.

It looks like Ian Botham after one spliff too many.

Isn't that Princess Anne, wearing an interesting hairdo? Afterwards, the hairdresser had to be destroyed.

She runs my local brothel – apparently.

ANSWERS

HAIR
Diego Maradona, who dyed his hair the colours of his football shirt – good job David Seaman hasn't had the same idea. Maradona was once caught in a hotel bedroom with a prostitute. He protested his innocence, calling it 'The Handjob of God'.

EYES
Prince Naseem Hamed, who isn't a real prince but is doing his best to live up to the image. He's got big ears and spends his evening waiting for an old bruiser to go down.

MOUTH
Monica Seles, who made her Wimbledon comeback last year. She was doing fine until Cliff Richard stood up and belted out 'Mack the Knife'.

HAIR
Karel Poborsky. When Manchester United first heard they'd got a Czech for 3.2 million pounds, they assumed someone had bought two shirts at the club shop.

EYES
Linford Christie, who was disqualified for False Starting in the Olympics, although he was quoted as saying he always goes 'on the B of Bang'. Considering all the children he's left scattered around London, that applies to his personal life too.

MOUTH
Michael Schumacher. Schumacher is of course German for 'cobblers'. Whereas Hill is English for 'cobblers'.

HAIR
Princess Anne, whose forte was the three-day event – a term used nowadays to describe a royal marriage.

EYES
Graeme Souness, who recently received £750,000 after the *Sunday People* compared him to a rat. The rat got a million.

MOUTH
Graham Taylor – a man whose greatest achievement was to bring obscure root vegetables to everyone's attention. By playing them in England's midfield.

The World of Formula One

Grand Prix racing is the fastest, sexiest, most glamorous sport on earth. So why not get off that sofa and join in? It's open to anyone with ambition, a competitive streak and about 50 million pounds.
Here are some of the things you will need:

1 x internationally recognised Formula One racing driver
£10 million

1 x unheard of Formula One racing driver with Brazilian name (will leave and join major team at first sign of success)
£2 million

2 x test drivers: probably one each of plucky Scottish rally driver who once won obscure European saloon-car race and floppy-haired public schoolboy from immensely wealthy family
£1 million

1 x useless Japanese driver (for obtaining Japanese finance only)
free

Assorted Brundles, Blundells, Rumbles and Trundles
£50,000 each

1 x fully race-tested, state-of-the-art F1 car
£15 million
(unless Arrows team)

1 x partially race-tested, slightly older, underpowered F1 car to ensure massive row between drivers during last part of season (if Arrows team, use as main car)
£10 million

1 x very shiny F1 car shell, to be sat on by bored drivers during promotional appearances in regional shopping precincts
£2 million

8 x competent race engineers to design and build reliable, competitive car which won't break down on lap 2
not available at this time

1 x pit crew – comprises:
  4 x blokes to do the work
  1 x bloke to hold sign saying 'brakes on'
  1 x bloke to hold umbrella over driver when wet
  1 x bloke to set himself on fire
  1 x bloke to lean into cockpit and shake head just before driver retires from race
  PLUS Some tools in pretty boxes with team name on
  Lots of brightly coloured overalls
£2 million

Blondes
approx. £50,000 each
price depends on age

1 x lawyer (to dispute minute and incomprehensible rule change)
£2 million

1 x race headquarters (selection of dull low-rise units on industrial estate in Oxfordshire, between sari warehouse and kosher bakery)
£10 per square foot

1 x belief that Formula One racing is even slightly interesting, a sport in any sense of the word or worthwhile in any way
apply Murray Walker for current price

Total   *approx.* **£50 million**

See over for full details of vehicle required

THE MODERN F1 CAR

Your step-by-step guide

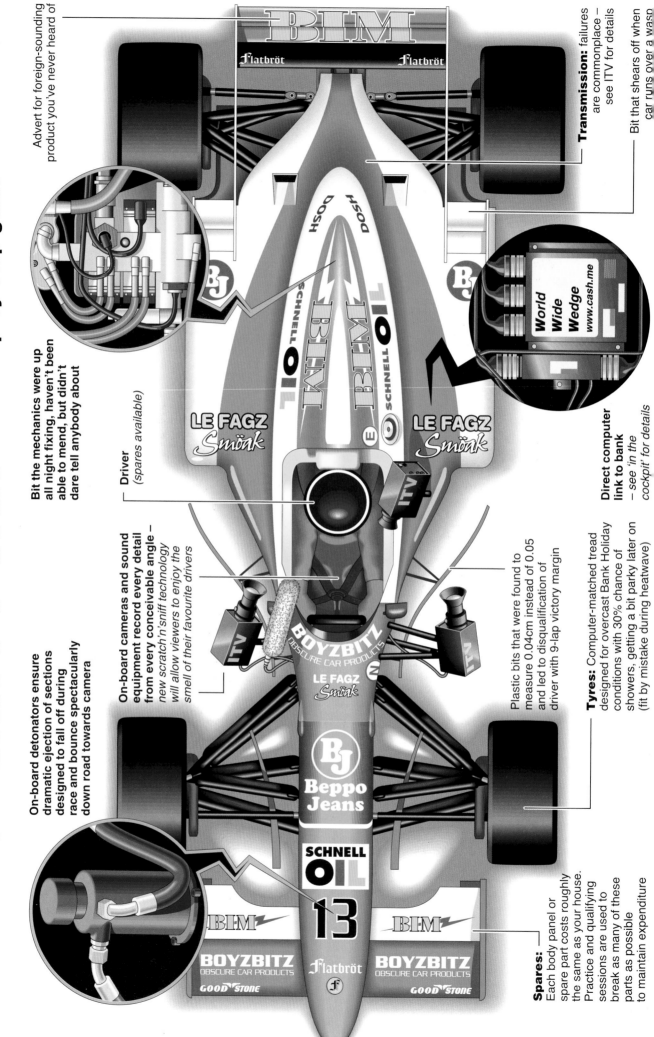

Advert for foreign-sounding product you've never heard of

Transmission: failures are commonplace – see ITV for details

Bit that shears off when car runs over a wasp

Bit the mechanics were up all night fixing, haven't been able to mend, but didn't dare tell anybody about

Driver *(spares available)*

Direct computer link to bank *– see 'in the cockpit' for details*

On-board detonators ensure dramatic ejection of sections designed to fall off during race and bounce spectacularly down road towards camera

On-board cameras and sound equipment record every detail from every conceivable angle – *new scratch'n'sniff technology will allow viewers to enjoy the smell of their favourite drivers*

Plastic bits that were found to measure 0.04cm instead of 0.05 and led to disqualification of driver with 9-lap victory margin

Tyres: Computer-matched tread designed for overcast Bank Holiday conditions with 30% chance of showers, getting a bit parky later on (fit by mistake during heatwave)

Spares: Each body panel or spare part costs roughly the same as your house. Practice and qualifying sessions are used to break as many of these parts as possible to maintain expenditure

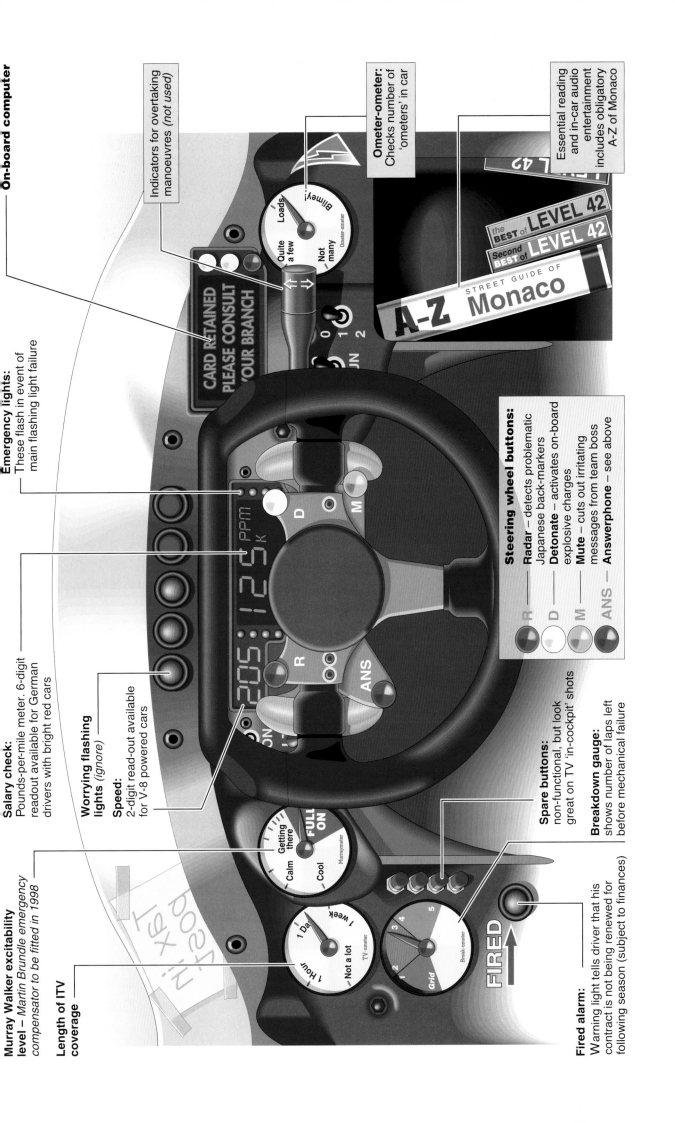

On-board computer

Indicators for overtaking manoeuvres *(not used)*

Ometer-ometer:
Checks number of 'ometers' in car

Essential reading and in-car audio entertainment includes obligatory A-Z of Monaco

Emergency lights:
These flash in event of main flashing light failure

Loads | Blimey!
Quite a few
Not many
Ometer-ometer

CARD RETAINED PLEASE CONSULT YOUR BRANCH

the BEST of LEVEL 42
Second BEST of LEVEL 42
STREET GUIDE OF A-Z Monaco

Salary check:
Pounds-per-mile meter. 6-digit readout available for German drivers with bright red cars

Worrying flashing lights *(ignore)*

Speed:
2-digit read-out available for V-8 powered cars

PPM
K

Steering wheel buttons:

R — **Radar** – detects problematic Japanese back-markers

D — **Detonate** – activates on-board explosive charges

M — **Mute** – cuts out irritating messages from team boss

ANS — **Answerphone** – see above

Murray Walker excitability level – *Martin Brundle emergency compensator to be fitted in 1998*

Length of ITV coverage

Getting there
Calm
Cool
FULL ON
Murraymeter

Spare buttons:
non-functional, but look great on TV 'in-cockpit' shots

Breakdown gauge:
shows number of laps left before mechanical failure

1 Hour
Not a lot
1 Day
1 week
TV-ometer

Grid
1 2 3 4 5
Break-ometer

Fired alarm:
Warning light tells driver that his contract is not being renewed for following season (subject to finances)

FIRED

colour by numbers

England goalkeeper David Seaman says 'Get your colouring pens out, readers, and colour in the jersey I so famously love to wear'.

Just fill in each area according to the colour chart opposite then get your big brother to draw a set of genitals on it in biro.

1 Vermilion
2 Puce
3 Day-glo orange
4 Night-glo orange
5 Something blue
6 Something borrowed
7 Something in the way she moves
8 Burnt sienna
9 Medium rare sienna
10 Matt emulsion
11 Matt busby
12 Matt bianco
13 Matt goss
14 Luke gloss
15 The other bloke
16 White
17 White with a hint of lemon
18 White with a hint of black (grey)
19 White with fish
20 Red with steak
21 Egg
22 Chocolate
23 Blood
24 Sweat
25 Tears
26 Semen
27 Black and blue
28 Equatorial Guinea
29 Sierra Leone
30 Moldova
31 Rutland
32 The Color Purple
33 Goose green
34 Robson green
35 Reverend green
36 Professor plum
37 Colonel mustard
38 Egg fried rice
39 Sweet and sour pork
40 Squid in its own ink
41 Squid in someone else's ink
42 Captain scarlet
43 Divine brown
44 Les gray
45 Rabbi lionel blue
46 I am curious yellow
47 Mr Pink
48 Mr Orange
49 Mr Tony Bennett
50 All of the above

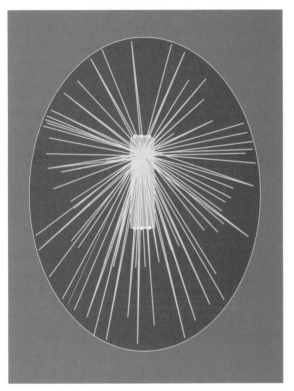

VIV RICHARDS
West Indies v England 1980-81 4th Test

DAVID GOWER
England v Pakistan 1992 5th Test

SPOT THE BALL

SPORT-WATCHING WITH RORY McGRATH

It's Sunday, and time to make an early start on a full day of TV sport. But it's not just a question of slumping in front of the TV – your every move should be meticulously planned. Stick to these simple guidelines and you won't go far wrong.

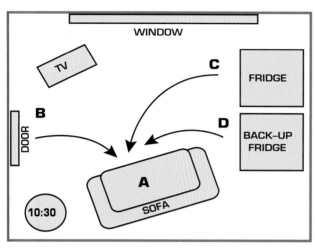

Station yourself horizontally on the sofa (A), having first secured a plentiful supply of pizzas from the deliveryman (B), beers from the fridge (C) and pork pies from the back-up fridge (D). Settle down to enjoy 'Monster Truck-Racing from Idaho' on Sky Sports 7.

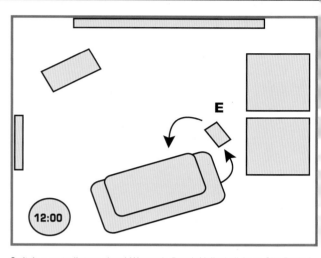

Switch over to 'International Women's Beach Volleyball from São Paulo.' Draw curtains and retrieve box of Kleenex (E) from below sofa. It's essential to keep fit in a gruelling all-day session of this kind.

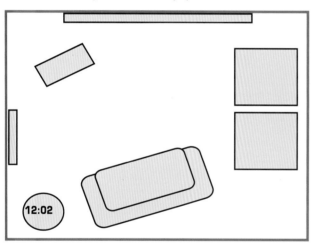

Finish watching beach volleyball, put away Kleenex and wait for heart rate to return to normal. Switch over to 'One Man And His Dog'. Spot particularly attractive-looking sheep; check curtains and retrieve Kleenex.

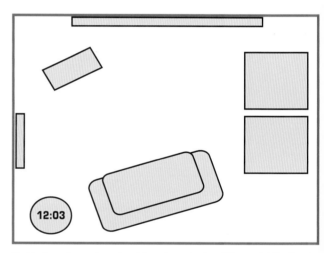

Suddenly realise you've missed three key minutes of the crucial Sky Sports build-up to the big match, just four hours away. Switch over to see Richard Keys speculate on the route the players' wives may take to the stadium. Spot particularly attractive wife...

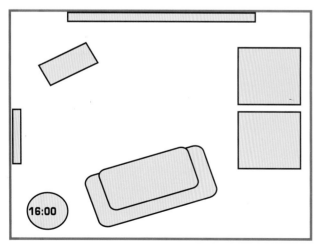

Kick-off. It's the big one. Arsenal v Leeds. How will Arsenal's watertight nine-man defence fare against the impregnable ten-man defence of Leeds? And what insightful gems will emerge from Barry Venison's half-time analysis?

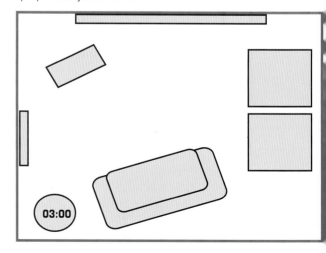

Wake up to humming noise and white dot on screen. Realise you've missed final 89 minutes of match as well as parents' golden anniversary dinner. Well done! Another successful day's sport watched the Rory McGrath way.

★ BEGINNER'S GUIDE TO
AMERICAN FOOTBALL

ARE YOU CONFUSED BY AMERICAN FOOTBALL? Does it just look like 22 men dressed as sofas running into each other at full speed? Simply remember the following basic points and soon you'll be able to follow every set play, turnover and touchdown with a thorough understanding of the world's no. 1 sport!

Atlanta Falcons' crunchbacker Bo 'The Dishwasher' Schwarzhof intercepts a two-up two-downer shuffled by the Broncos' back flipper John 'The Baptist' Heidegger.

PLAYERS

Each team has two linebackers, two wide receivers, a tight end, a loose end, a new beginning, three backscratchers, a quarter pounder and a rush goalie.

THE FIELD

The area between the end lines and the inbound lines is the home defence zone. The area between the outward bound lines and the ley lines is the clone zone. The leg zone is connected to the knee zone – hear the word of the Lord.

TACTICS

If you jacksie a sky-higher to centre-left with a prelim still on the board, you're guaranteed a run-in with a hedgehog in limbo. The career record is of course 13/2 under 72 in '72.

Always remember to double-eye your lowball with a rush to the fly-line. In this instance, the tight-end with the loose helmet is prone to tackle-grope.

Nothing beats a half-clincher in the field zone, as the trouserpress lines off on 27th and Broadway. This guarantees an apple turnover on the 10 by 8 with an RSJ, sucking out all the juices.

THE FINAL COUNTDOWN

Holding the lead by scouring the pads till they come out nice and shiny means your clingbacker can go through route 128 down by the powerline, going faster miles an hour.

Chico 'Childfondler' Rodriguez of the New England Patriots downsizes a hundred-yard fundament in the ninth quarter of the second hoedown at the Barbara Z. Cartland megabowl.

Ed 'Reader's Wives' Jablonsky, wide longhopper of the New York Giants, defends a defensive offence pitched by the 49ers' deeply offensive backfield, Lou 'Importer of Animal Porn' Bruckheimer.

PROGRAMME GUIDE

A complete list of the transmission dates and guests from the first 4 series of 'They Think It's All Over', plus the 'No Holds Barred' video. Total number of shows: 30.

SERIES ONE

NO.	DATE	GUESTS	FEEL THE SPORTSMAN	GARY'S SCORE	DAVID'S SCORE
1	14/9/95	Roger Black Rory Bremner	Willie Carson Giant Haystacks	23	17
2	21/9/95 23/9/95	Tessa Sanderson Clive Anderson	Eddie Edwards John McCririck	18	21
3	28/9/95 30/9/95	John Barnes Jo Brand	Geoff Capes Lucinda Green	17	25
4	5/10/95 7/10/95	Barry McGuigan Fred MacAulay	David Shepherd Mickey Skinner	19	14
5	12/10/95 14/10/95	John Motson Alistair McGowan	John Motson Jack Russell	26	25
6	19/10/95 21/10/95	Ally McCoist Hugh Dennis	Willie Thorne Aylesbury FC	18	18
			SERIES SCORE:	121	120

Gary won 3 programmes to David's 2, with one tied. However, the series was awarded to David after Gary and Rory confessed to cheating during the Feel the Sportsman round by attempting to make holes in their blindfolds with needles.

CHRISTMAS SPECIAL

	DATE	GUESTS	FEEL THE SPORTSMAN	GARY	DAVID
	28/12/95 30/12/95	Allan Lamb Mel Smith	Duncan Goodhew Gareth Chilcott	16	15

SERIES TWO

NO.	DATE	GUESTS	FEEL THE SPORTSMAN	GARY'S SCORE	DAVID'S SCORE
1	12/3/96 16/3/96	Ian Wright Neil Morrissey	Vinnie Jones GB bobsleigh team	16	15
2	19/3/96 23/3/96	Sharron Davies Bob Mills	Subbuteo Gary Lineker Derek Redmond	15	15

Tie-break won by Gary after guessing, more accurately, the number of times Ray Parlour said 'obviously' in an interview.

| 3 | 26/3/96 | Steve Cram | England basketball team | 17 | 17 |
| | 30/3/96 | Craig Charles | Trevor Brooking | | |

Tie-break won by David after Gary failed to answer a question from the quiz book which he allegedly wrote.

4	2/4/96	Kriss Akabusi	Simon Smith (sumo wrestler)	19	11
	6/4/96	John Gordon Sinclair	Eric Hall		
5	9/4/96	Steve Davis	Mick the Miller RIP (greyhound)	18	19
	13/4/96	Gaby Roslin	Striker the Dog (US World Cup mascot)		
6	16/4/96 20/4/96	Teddy Sheringham Frank Skinner	Greg Rusedski William 'The Refrigerator' Perry	20	20

Tie-break won by Gary after David failed to remember who really wrote 'David Gower's Quiz Book'.

| 7 | 23/4/96
27/4/96 | Rob Wainwright
Tony Hawks | Steve Backley
Henry Cooper | 19 | 19 |
| | | | SERIES SCORE: | 123 | 118 |

Series tie-break won by David in a game of paper, scissors and stone.

| | | | David won the series | 4-3. | |

SERIES THREE

NO.	DATE	GUESTS	FEEL THE SPORTSMAN	GARY'S SCORE	DAVID'S SCORE
1	12/9/96 14/9/96	Ian Walker Gordon Kennedy	Johnny Herbert Jane Sixsmith	22	17
2	19/9/96	Jimmy 'Fivebellies' Gardner	Eric Bristow	23	21
	21/9/96	Alistair McGowan	Redgrave & Pinsent		
3	26/9/96	Kelly Holmes	Victor Ubogu	18	16
	28/9/96	Curtis Walker	GB beach volleyball team		
4	3/10/96	Brian Moore	Oliver Skeete	20	23
	5/10/96	Mark Little	Peter Shilton		
5	10/10/96	Chris Waddle	Martin Offiah (rugby league)	15	19
	12/10/96	Jo Brand	Martin Offiah (rugby union)		
6	17/10/96 19/10/96	Dermot Reeve Mark Hurst	Dennis Taylor Dominic Cork	17	15

SERIES THREE (continued)

NO.	DATE	GUESTS	FEEL THE SPORTSMAN	GARY	DAVID
7	24/10/96	Nick Owen	Rachael Heyhoe-Flint	20	18
	26/10/96	Phill Jupitus	Linford Christie (waxwork)		
			SERIES SCORE:	135	129
			Gary won the series	5-2.	

CHRISTMAS SPECIAL

	DATE	GUESTS	FEEL THE SPORTSMAN	GARY	DAVID
	23/12/96 28/12/96	Steve Backley David Baddiel	Lee Hurst (footballer) The Red Devils	25	20

SERIES FOUR

NO.	DATE	GUESTS	FEEL THE SPORTSMAN	GARY'S SCORE	DAVID'S SCORE
1	9/4/97	Phil Tufnell	British synchronised swimming team	20	24
	12/4/97	Alan Davies	Chesterfield FC		
2	16/4/97 19/4/97	Steve Collins Tony Hawks	Bob Nudd Neil Adams	18	11
3	23/4/97 26/4/97	Dave Bassett Mark Little	Tony Bullimore Arsenal Ladies FC	17	15
4	30/4/97 3/5/97	Brough Scott Stephen Fry	Cambridge boat crew David Elleray	19	18
5	7/5/97 10/5/97	Denise Lewis Jeff Green	4 x 400 relay team Peter Collins	20	14
6	14/5/97	Matthew Pinsent	J M Littman (British sled dog champion)	16	19
	17/5/97	Julian Clary	Stirling Moss		
7	21/5/97 24/5/97	Ron Atkinson Zoe Ball	Tony Allcock Richard Dunwoody	17	20
			SERIES SCORE:	127	121
			Gary won the series	4-3.	

'THEY THINK IT'S ALL OVER – NO HOLDS BARRED' VIDE

GUESTS	FEEL THE SPORTSMAN	GARY'S SCORE	DAVID'S SC
Roger Black Neil Morrissey	Harold 'Dickie' Bird Fanny Sunesson	20	21

SPORTS DAY EVENTS

Egg and Spoon Race	Times
Gower	8.68
McGrath	10.44
Lineker	12.56
Hurst	21.02

Three-legged Race	Times
Hurst	11.96 (same time all)
Lineker	
Gower	
McGrath	

After a lot of whingeing, Hurst was placed first, Lineker second, Gower third and McGrath fourth – a first for the three-legged race.

Egg Catching	Distance
Lineker	100 ft (World record)
Hurst	60 ft
Gower	50 ft
McGrath	30 ft

Obstacle Race	Times
Hurst	1-30.23
Lineker	1-33.79
Gower	1-58.07
McGrath	1-58.42

Sack Race	Times
Lineker	16.80
Gower	18.37
McGrath	19.82
Hurst	20.95

Individual Result
1. Lineker – 16
2. =Gower – 13
2. =Hurst – 13
4. McGrath – 8

Team Result
Gower and Hurst – 26
Lineker and McGrath – 24

One point was carried through to Gower an Hurst's total, which proved crucial in their overall victory.

LEAGUE TABLE

	P	W	D	L	F	A	Pts
GARY	30	15	5	10	567	544	50
DAVID	30	10	5	15	544	567	35

By a strange quirk, all 4 tie-breaks in the show's history took place in the second series, although one drawn game in series one occurred before tie-breaks had been introduced.

Only Jo Brand and Alistair McGowan have been on the TV show twice, although Roger Black and Neil Morrissey were invited back for the 'No Holds Barred' video.

STATISTICAL BREAKDOWN

Final Scores
The lowest final score is 11 (by David, twice) and the highest is 26 (by Gary). Gary's lowest score is 15 (3 times). The most common final totals are 17 and 20 (each score having been reached 9 times).

Gary has finished on 20 no less than 6 times (a ratio of 1 in 5), yet this didn't happen until the 13th programme, making the ratio since then a remarkable 1 in 3.

Over half the individual team scores have been between 17 and 20 (34 out of 60), with exactly two-thirds of Gary's totals being between these figures (20 out of 30).

Overall
In 30 shows, Gary has scored 567 points to David's 544. In each of the four series, Gary has scored more points overall than David, this despite Gary's 33 point lead working out as only 1.1 points per match. In fact, if you take scores per programme over the 4 series, the average result is 18.90 to Gary and 18.13 to David.

'Little Urchin Lee'

As dawn breaks, Little Urchin Lee wakes on his straw pallet in the pea-soup fog of London's traditional East End and rubs the sleep from his eyes. Setting out through the cobbled dawn, keeping to the main streets to avoid Jack the Ripper, this cheeky chappie trots off to work with a cheerful grin on his little bald face. All around, the traditional costermonger cries of old London can be heard: 'Buy my lovely apples!', 'Car stereo for sale!', 'Join the BNP!', 'You try living next door to 'em!' Soon he reaches his destination – the old manor house, where he will spend the rest of his short life with his bald head rammed up a dank soot-filled chimney.

Now this pleasing image has been captured for all time by Taiwanese master potsman U Bai Tat. His immaculate handiwork has been reproduced in a limited edition (2.5 million) and can be yours for the convenient price of just £2.99.*

* not the real price

Little Urchin Lee comes with genuine 3-carat crystal working parts and mad staring eyes. Pull the string and he talks incessantly on any subject. (Note: there is no 'off' string.)

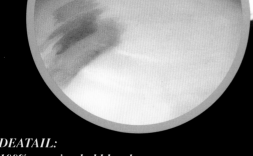

DEATAIL:
100% genuine bald head

THE

They think
it's all
over

ANNUAL

was written by Simon Bullivant,
Bill Matthews, Jim Pullin,
Pete Sinclair, Robert Fraser Steele
and Harry Thompson

BBC BOOKS

IN ASSOCIATION WITH
TALKBACK PRODUCTIONS LIMITED